GOOD HUMOR

God's Kids Say the Funniest Things

THE BEST JOKES AND CARTOONS FROM

The Joyful Noiseletter

EDITED BY CAL AND ROSE SAMRA

BARBOUR
PUBLISHING

Published in association with *The Joyful Noiseletter* by Barbour Publishing, Inc., P.O. Box 719, Uhrichsville, Ohio 44683, www.barbourbooks.com

To purchase additional copies of this book, please see your local Christian bookstore or contact Barbour Publishing at the address or website noted above.

Our mission is to publish and distribute inspirational products offering exceptional value and biblical encouragement to the masses.

Printed in the United States of America.

TO OUR GRANDDAUGHTERS,
MADELINE, KATE, AND LIZZIE,
WITH THANKS FOR THE SOUND OF
YOUR CONTAGIOUS LAUGHTER.

To me a smile is no sin, and a laugh is no crime. I never knew what the hearty laugh and what the happy face meant till I knew Christ.

Charles H. Spurgeon
English Baptist Preacher

Contents

Preface

Humorist Erma Bombeck wrote that she once sat in church in a pew behind a small child who kept turning around and smiling at other people. He wasn't misbehaving. He was just smiling.

Finally, his mother jerked him about, gave him a belt, and said, "Stop that grinning! You're in church!" Then she returned to her prayers, leaving the child in tears.

"Suddenly, I was angry," Erma wrote. "I wanted to grab this child with the tear-stained face close to me and tell him about my God. The happy God. The smiling God. The God who had to have a sense of humor to create the likes of us .... If this child couldn't smile in church, where was there left to go?"

Children, especially, were attracted to Jesus and crowded around him. Children generally are not attracted to gloomy or stern personalities. This was no gloomy Messiah.

"Let the little children come to me,
and do not hinder them, for the kingdom
of God belongs to such as these."
MARK 10:14

He called a little child to him, and placed the child among them. And he said: "Truly I tell you, unless you change and become like little children, you will never enter the kingdom of heaven. Therefore, whoever takes the lowly position of this child is the greatest in the kingdom of heaven."
MATTHEW 18:2–4

For the past twenty-five years, *The Joyful Noiseletter* has provided subscribing churches with jokes that pastors can tell and rib-tickling humor and cartoons which are reproducible in local church newsletters, bulletins, and websites. One of our most popular regular columns is "God's Kids Say the Funniest Things."

This book features some of *TJN*'s best jokes, anecdotes, and cartoons about kids from past issues, and we appreciate the Pauline zeal of Paul M. Miller in helping to organize them. The copyrighted materials in this book are just for laughs, and may not be reproduced in church publications and websites.

But subscribers to *The Joyful Noiseletter* have automatic permission to reproduce the jokes, humor, and cartoons in each issue of the newsletter in their local church publication and websites. An annual subscription is $29, and may be ordered from *TJN*'s website (www.joyfulnoiseletter.com) or by calling toll-free 1-800-877-2757.

Good cheer! Enjoy!

CAL SAMRA, EDITOR
THE JOYFUL NOISELETTER

"I put Mrs. Schmidt in my prayers last
night – but I see she's still here."

Introduction

Sit long enough around the table at a family meal,
and as sure as anything, little Willy will spill his
milk, which in turn will remind a smarmy rela-
tive of something clever said by her grandson at
Uncle Charlie's birthday dinner, which in turn
provides the opportunity for an onslaught of
kiddie tales, both true and highly hyperbolized.

"Did I tell you what Junior's teacher told me
that he told her about our family?"

Then there are the annual holiday letters
that update kith and kin on Sally's teacher's
evaluation of the five-year-old's IQ (probably a

throwback from Mom's side of the family) and what the piano recital audience thought of her rendition of "By a Wigwam."

"Stop me if I told you this before, but you'll never believe how Lisa told the story of Adam and Eve to her Bible class the other day."

So while we chuckle and gloat over the cute *bon mots* and unknowing wise observations of our children, the good Lord looks down and smiles, remembering how He placed humor high on the list of requirements for His kids. If you hang around your church clergy long enough, or listen to classroom teachers, or keep your ears open at any gathering that involves human beings, you'll have to agree, God's kids do say the funniest things.

THE FAMILY CIRCUS
by Bil & Jeff Keane

"Is it okay to pray before the test if I don't do it out loud?"

from *JoyfulNoiseletter.com*
© Bil Keane.

"Guess What I. . .Today?"

God's Kids at School

When you say good-bye to them in the morning, who knows what indicting words are going to come out of their mouths! More than one teacher has told a parent, "Promise! I won't believe what Junior said about your family, if you promise not to believe everything Junior reports on what happened in class today."

It's not much different in Sunday school—only the topic of study has been changed.

Hooray for Snow Days!

A heavy snowstorm closed the schools in one town. When the children returned to school a few days later, one teacher asked her grade-schoolers whether they had used the time away from school constructively.

"I sure did, teacher," one little girl replied. "I just prayed for more snow."

CATHERINE HALL
PITTSBURGH, PENNSYLVANIA

What about Grammar?

A teacher in a seventh-grade class in Kings Mountain, North Carolina, asked her pupils to write a short statement on what each wished to become in life. One pupil submitted this:

"Be what you is and not what you ain't. Cause if you ain't what you is, you is what you ain't."

JOAN N. HARRIS
SILER CITY, NORTH CAROLINA

That's Right!

A soccer ball, kicked through the window of a classroom where there was a program for small children at Corinth Reformed Church in Hickory, North Carolina, created some havoc.

So instead of assigning a Bible verse to memorize in advance of the next meeting, the teacher instructed the children to memorize any verse and earn a treat.

The next week, six-year-old Timmy was at a loss to remember any verse. After some encouragement from the teacher, he finally exclaimed: "I know! I know! 'In God we trust!'"

PASTOR BOB THOMPSON
HICKORY, NORTH CAROLINA

And He Will

A six-year-old boy came home from a church school and asked his mother if it was all right to ask God to help him.

"Of course," she replied. "Is there something worrying you?"

"No," he said, "but at school today my teacher said that if I interrupted her one more time, 'May God help you.'"

JEFF TOTTEN
LAKE CHARLES, LOUISIANA

Peace in Any Language

An elementary school teacher was reviewing antonyms with her gifted first-grade and second-grade classes. She asked one of the boys for an antonym for "war."

When he couldn't come up with a word, the teacher offered a hint: "When I go to church on Sundays, my minister always prays for world *peace*, the opposite of *war*. Does your pastor pray for peace?"

"I don't know," the student replied, "because my church prays in tongues."

SMILEY ANDERS
BATON ROUGE (LOUISIANA) *ADVOCATE*

Seasonal Answers

A third-grade teacher at Mercer County Elementary School in Kentucky compiled an exam consisting of twenty questions for her students. One of the questions: "List in any order the four seasons."

Sixty-seven percent of the students gave the following answer: "(1) squirrel season; (2) deer season; (3) rabbit season; (4) UK basketball season."

CHARLES GARRETT
FORT GAINES, GEORGIA

Fourth-Grade Spirit

While visiting the fourth-grade class at our parochial school, I noticed a pair of parakeets, which were class pets. Thinking this might be a teachable moment about the Holy Spirit—the Paraclete—I asked the students who could tell me the difference between parakeets and Paraclete.

One girl raised her hand and answered enthusiastically: "Parakeets are birds, paracletes are soccer shoes."

REV. ALEX B. CYMERMAN
HOLYOKE, MASSACHUSETTS

A Ten-Year-Old's Question

Dr. Ron Lavin of San Diego, California, has written his twenty-fourth book, titled *Only the Lonely (Another Look at Loneliness)*, published by CSS Publishing House, Lima, Ohio. Here's a choice anecdote from the book:

A Sunday school teacher asked her class, "What is the last book in the Bible?"

Johnny, a ten-year-old boy, answered, "The book of Revolution."

"That's Revelation, not revolution," the teacher replied.

The following Sunday, the teacher said, "I've been thinking all week about Johnny's answer. The last book of the Bible is Revelation, but it is a kind of revolutionary book. As a matter of fact, the whole Bible is revolutionary. Does anyone know who wrote the last book of the Bible?"

Johnny's hand went up, and he asked, "Was it Paul Revere?"

Not the Holy Spurt

On the first day of junior high school, the English teacher asked the class to write a one-sentence statement about their goals for the year. That evening, the teacher (a fellow church member) called one boy's mother and told her that her son had written, "My goal for the year is to grow in spirit."

Flushed with pride, the mother told her son about it. The boy replied, "Mom, the teacher misread what I wrote. I didn't say to grow in spirit. I said to get my growing spurt."

CURTIS ANDERSON
FORT WORTH, TEXAS
FORT WORTH (TEXAS) *STAR TELEGRAM*

Wonders

After a geography class studied the Seven Wonders of the World, the students were asked to list what they considered were the Seven Wonders of the World. They voted for (1) Egypt's Great Pyramids, (2) Taj Mahal, (3) Grand Canyon, (4) Panama Canal, (5) Empire State Building, (6) St. Peter's Basilica, (7) China's Great Wall.

A girl took some extra time with her list then told the teacher, "I think the Seven Wonders of the World are (1) to touch, (2) to taste, (3) to see, (4) to hear, (5) to run, (6) to laugh, and (7) to love."

LOIS WARD
GLEAMINGS

Proverb Insights

A fourth-grade teacher gave each child in her class the first half of a well-known proverb, and asked them to complete the proverb. Here are some of the answers:

- "It's always darkest before. . .daylight savings time."

- "An idle mind is. . .the best way to relax."

- "Better to be safe than. . .punch a sixth grader."

- "If you lie down with dogs. . .you'll stink in the morning."

- "Laugh and the whole world laughs with you, cry and. . .you have to blow your nose."

HARRIET M. ADAMS
MORTON, PENNSYLVANIA

Test of Time

A mother overheard her little girl praying:

"Now I lay me down to rest.
I pray I pass tomorrow's test.
If I should die before I wake,
That's one less test I'll have to take."

GEORGE GOLDTRAP
ORMOND-BY-THE-SEA, FLORIDA

From Grade Two

Second graders are the best theologians? Here's several discussions between second graders about Jesus and the Holy Ghost:

First second grader: "Well, one thing I never figured out is if Jesus is God, why did He let Himself be killed?"

Second second grader: "Silly, it's because He loves us, and He died for us!"

Third second grader: "Yeah, and not only did He die, but He came back three days later!"

Fourth second grader: "Well, all I know is that when He came back He was really smart!"

Teacher: "Why do you think He was so smart?"

Fourth second grader: "Because when He did come back, He came back as the Holy Ghost, and everyone knows you can't kill a ghost. He wasn't taking any more chances. He never wanted to go through that again!"

BRENDA BRISTOL
COLCHESTER, VERMONT

OK in the UK

The pupils at Cheam School, one of the most re-spected boys' schools in England, were being briefed for the expected visit next day of Lord Geoffrey Fisher, the archbishop of Canterbury. They were told, "If the archbishop speaks to you, you must address him as either 'My Lord,' or 'Your Grace.'"

When the distinguished cleric arrived complete with gaiters, the boys were marshaled in a row, shoes shined and cheeks scrubbed. The archbishop walked along the line smiling and stopped to speak to one boy. "How old are you, sonny?" he asked.

The boy spoke up: "My God, I'm ten!"

SHERWOOD ELIOT WIRT
THE BOOK OF JOY

Science Exam

Actual answer on a children's science exam:

Question: How do you delay milk turning sour?
Answer: Keep it in the cow.

Welcome Back to School!

Sampling of test blunders collected by Richard Benson in his book *F, in Exams: The Funniest Test Paper Blunders:*

Question: What is nitrate?
Answer: Much cheaper than a day rate.

Question: What did Mahatma Gandhi and Genghis Khan have in common?
Answer: Unusual names.

Question: Name only one of the early Romans' greatest achievements.
Answer: Learning to speak Latin.

Question: Where was the American Declaration of Independence signed?
Answer: At the bottom.

Question: What is a fibula?
Answer: A little lie.

Question: Explain the phrase "free press."
Answer: When your mom irons trousers for you.

Question: Name the wife of Orpheus, whom he attempted to save from the underworld.
Answer: Mrs. Orpheus.

Music Hath Charms. . .

Bud Frimoth of Portland, Oregon, passed on these actual answers from students on their musical exams:

- ☼ "*Refrain* means don't do it. A refrain in music is the part you'd better not try to sing."

- ☼ "Gregorian chant has no music, just singers singing the same lines."

- ☼ "Music sung by two people at the same time is called a duel; if they sing without music, it is called Acapulco."

- ☼ "A virtuoso is a musician with real high morals."

- ☼ "Probably the most marvelous fugue was the one between the Hatfields and the McCoys."

- ☼ "Sherbert composed the Unfinished Symphony."

- ☼ "Rock Monanoff was a famous composer of piano concerti."

Definition Needed

Jamie LeJeune went to school on her first day at Holy Family Catholic Church School in Port Allen, Louisiana. When her mom, Jennifer LeJeune, asked her how her first day went, Jamie replied that everything went just fine, with the exception of one problem: "They don't have enough 'hookers' at school."

Jamie's mom and dad were relieved when Jamie explained that she had no place to hang her backpack due to the "hooker" shortage.

SMILEY ANDERS
BATON ROUGE (LOUISIANA) *ADVOCATE*

End Times Hope

Graphically describing the Day of Judgment, a preacher declared: "There will be great earthquakes and floods. Thunder will crash and lightning will set fires and scorch much of the earth. People will run in every direction, but there will be no escape. Then darkness will fall over the earth."

A little boy sitting in the back pew asked his mother: "Do you suppose they'll let school out early?"

CATHERINE HALL

Classroom PC

A sixth grader stood up in class and gave this politically correct report of the origins of the Thanksgiving holiday:

"The pilgrims came here seeking freedom of you know what.

"When they landed, they gave thanks to you know who.

"Because of them, we can worship each Sunday, you know where."

REV. KARL R. KRAFT
MANTUA, NEW JERSEY

Smart Alecks

Actual answers to children's science exam:

Question: Name the four seasons.
Answer: Salt, pepper, mustard, and vinegar.

Question: How is dew formed?
Answer: The sun shines down on the leaves and makes them perspire.

Question: What does the word "benign" mean?
Answer: Benign is what you will be after you be eight.

PROF. RISE SAMRA
BARRY UNIVERSITY MIAMI, FLORIDA

"Did Pastor Get His New Car from All the Money in the Collection Plate?"

God's Kids and Practicality

Kids have such a great way of uncomplicating life. Whether it's an ethical issue, stewardship, or. . . Speaking of stewardship, we've all faced it—it's a quiet moment during worship; there's a holy hush over the congregation which is suddenly shattered when Junior spies his dad writing out his offering check and exclaims for all to hear, "Boy, Dad, you spent more than that on sis's Girl Scout cookies!" It's kind of a black-and-white world to God's kids.

The Awe-Full Truth

One Sunday morning, before the beginning of mass, I asked a group of children, "What do you have to do to get to heaven?"

One young theologian yelled at the top of his voice, "Ya gotta die!"

FR. GREGORY CHAMBERLAIN, OSB
EVANSVILLE, INDIANA

Remember the Fatted Calf

The children in Sunday school were reading the story of the prodigal son. The teacher asked one little girl which character in the story faced the most difficult challenge.

"The fatted calf, 'cause he got killed," she replied.

JEFF TOTTEN

The Truth about Aging

Three little sisters were talking very excitedly about their upcoming vacation to Michigan's Upper Peninsula, and crossing the Mackinac Bridge. The youngest girl, Lizzie, age five, began crying and ran into the arms of her mother.

Her mother asked her why she was crying, and Lizzie said she was "scared to go over that long, high bridge."

"But you went over that bridge when you were a baby, and you weren't scared then," her mother said.

Lizzie replied through her tears, "When you're a baby, you don't know stuff. When you're older, you know stuff."

The Liturgical Hop

When my three-year-old grandson came back from church, I asked the boy, "What did you do in church?"

Accompanying it with the appropriate movements, he replied, "Up and down, up and down, up and down!"

HECTOR HAMMERLY
VANCOUVER, BRITISH COLUMBIA

That's Final!

Little Jack, a four-year-old boy in our prekinder-garten class, was chosen to be baby Jesus in the Christmas pageant. He was very proud and did a wonderful job.

Later, when his family was explaining Good Friday to him, he got very upset and said, "I was baby Jesus, but they are not getting me up on any cross."

FR. FRANK WEBER
CLIFTON, NEW JERSEY

Mom Knows Best

Fr. Don Cleary of Omaha, Nebraska, was pre-paring a group of children for regular confession. "I wanted to talk about the 'examination of con-science' through which a penitent recalls his or her sins," the priest recalled. "So I began by ask-ing the children, 'How do you know your sins?'"

"I expected someone to answer, 'I examine my conscience.' Instead, one child answered, 'I ask my mother.'"

In All Modesty

One evening shortly after the funeral service of her beloved uncle, eight-year-old Julia "JuJu" Salamey, daughter of Hanan and Mike Salamey of Saginaw, Michigan, remarked: "Uncle Emile is still with us; he watches everything we do—except when we go to the bathroom, he stands outside the door."

A Practical Solution

When our son, Christopher, was a toddler, he loved to watch his "Jesus videos." But he was upset by one of the videos, which showed Jesus overturning the tables in the Temple and telling the people to leave.

Christopher said, "I don't like it when He does that. He looks mad." I tried to explain to him that Jesus said, "My house is a house of prayer," and that by doing those things in the Temple, people were not respecting God's house.

Christopher replied, "I know what they could have done instead! Why didn't they just have a yard sale?"

DEBBIE HEISEY
MANHEIM, PENNSYLVANIA

Quite a Pair

A Sunday school teacher asked her class of small children: "What was the name of Jesus' mother?"

"Mary," a little girl answered.

"And what was the name of Jesus' father?" the teacher asked.

"A little boy raised his hand and replied, "Verge."

"Where on earth did you come up with that?" the teacher asked.

"Well, you know, they're always talking about 'Verge 'n' Mary,'" the boy said.

LOWELL YODER
HOLLAND, OHIO

Come On In

A woman and her eight-year-old daughter drove past a church having a fall festival. The mother wondered out loud if the church's festival was only for the congregation.

Her little daughter replied, "We can go in, Mom. The sign says 'All Saints Church.'"

MINNEAPOLIS STAR TRIBUNE

Who Else?

A Sunday school teacher was discussing with her class of youngsters the difference between right and wrong, "As an example," she said, "if I get into a man's pocket and take money from his wallet, what would I be?"

A little boy raised his hand and answered: "You'd be his wife!"

Sibling Solution

A Sunday school teacher was discussing the commandment, "Honor thy father and thy mother," with her eight-year-old children. She asked, "Is there a commandment that tells us how to treat our brothers and sisters?"

"Yeah," a boy replied. "Thou shalt not kill."

GEORGE GOLDTRAP

Good Answer

A father asked his son what was the highest number he had counted to. The boy replied, "Nine hundred and seventy-three."

The father asked the boy why he had stopped there. The boy replied, "Because church was over."

HOLLY SUTULA

Night-Night

A four-year-old girl was having trouble sleeping at night, waking up because she was afraid. Each time her mother tucked her back into bed, and reminded her that Jesus was with her and would keep her safe.

But the sleepless nights continued, and the little girl sought comfort in her parents' bedroom. Finally, one night the mother asked her if she had prayed for Jesus to take her fear away and help her fall asleep.

"Yes, I did," the girl replied. "He told me to come get you."

REV. KARL R. KRAFT

Collection Insight

The deacons were passing the offering plate when a small voice rang out, "Hey, Dad, you don't have to pay for me 'cause I'm still under five."

PASTOR DONALD PROUT
WEST PRESTON, VICTORIA, AUSTRALIA

Jake's Ear

Jake, the young son of a friend of mine, had an ear infection which was affecting his hearing, so his mother took him to the doctor. The doctor asked, "Jake, which ear is it?"

Jake replied, "Two thousand five."

REV. DR. GEOFF PANKHURST
TOOWOOMBA, AUSTRALIA

Dads' Cut

Three children were overheard bragging about their fathers. An investment counselor's son said, "My father makes sixty dollars an hour just sitting at his desk."

A lawyer's son replied, "My dad talks on the phone for thirty minutes and makes one hundred and twenty-five dollars."

The pastor's son laughed, "That's nothing! My father preaches for fifteen minutes, and it takes four men to collect all the money!"

EDWARD MORRIS
WEST ISLIP, NEW YORK

No Guarantee

I took my three-year-old son to the church for the first time. When the ushers passed the basket for the offerings, he was amazed and watched quizzically. Later in the service, when the congregation went to the front to receive communion, he said in a very loud voice, "Mom, are they going up to get their money back?"

BERNITA HOY
CHANHASSEN, MINNESOTA
MINNEAPOLIS STAR TRIBUNE

Hmmm. . .

From papers written by grade-school students:

☼ "Syntax is all money collected at church from sinners."

☼ "The climate is hottest next to the Creator."

MARY AHLRICH
BLOOMINGTON, ILLINOIS

Money's Worth

After church one Sunday morning, a mother commented: "The choir was awful this morning."

The father commented: "The sermon was too long."

Their seven-year-old girl added: "You've got to admit it was a pretty good show for a dime."

JOE MAHER
OXNARD, CALIFORNIA

Spick-and-Span

Our three young grandchildren were playing with face paints and left the bathroom quite colorful but messy. Their mother said they must clean it up.

Her five-year-old daughter replied, "Don't worry, Mommy. When I was upstairs, I prayed that it would be clean tomorrow."

LORRAINE OLSEN HALL
LAKEVILLE, MINNESOTA
MINNEAPOLIS STAR TRIBUNE

"Oh, My"

On a recent Sunday, the highlight of the holy baptism turned out not to be the sprinkling of water, nor the anointing with oil, nor even the lovely baby himself, but rather his older (age three) brother's loud exclamation as a candle was lit: "Uh-oh! That's gonna hurt!"

DR. ALAN STEWART
WILMINGTON, DELAWARE

Who's a Mammal?

My daughter, Bailey, was all excited about learning about bats in her kindergarten class. She came home with a list of bat facts.

We were talking about these bat facts when she said, "Mom, did you know that we're mammals, too?"

Her all-knowing sister, Lily, who was listening, piped in with, "We're not mammals! We're Christians!"

SONJA GELLA
EDEN PRAIRIE, MINNESOTA

Plastic, Thanks

My four-year-old grandson, Nicholas, attends preschool at his home church in Ennis, Texas. At Thanksgiving time, the teacher asked if anyone would like to pray. Nicholas volunteered and prayed:

"Dear God, thank You for my school and my teacher and my friends. Thank You for my mother and daddy, and thank You for credit cards so we can buy things."

OWEN PHILLIPS
FORT WORTH (TEXAS) *STAR-TELEGRAM*

That Uncle Melvin. . .

A day before the funeral of his Uncle Melvin, young Cody (age six) was asked to say grace at the table at dinnertime. He did so in fine order and concluded with: "And help Uncle Melvin behave in heaven!"

PASTOR STEVE HARTMAN
NORMAL, ILLINOIS

"That's All Folks!"

During his children's sermon, Pastor Drew Preston, youth minister at Maize Road Baptist Church in Columbus, Ohio, asked the youngsters "why we say 'Amen' at the close of our prayers."

A youngster promptly answered, "That means 'Over and out.'"

DOC GOODWIN
COLUMBUS, OHIO

Practical Advice

After Sunday school, a grandmother was testing her grandson to see if he had learned the names of the New Testament writers. She asked the boy about the fisherman, the tax collector, the physician. . .and each time the boy answered correctly.

Finally, the boy said impatiently: "Grandma, I think you should try to figure out some of these for yourself."

GEORGE GOLDTRAP

TV or No TV

My son, Mark, four, was very excited that the Easter Bunny would be coming to our house. I asked him if he knew what Easter was really about.

He quickly replied, "Jesus died on the cross, so we can live with Him in heaven some day. But I don't want to die."

I said he didn't have to die right now, but everyone will die sometime.

He said, "Okay, but if there's no TV in heaven, I'm leaving."

JENNY ORESHNICK
BLAINE, MINNESOTA

Oh, Yeah?

In church, a father gave his four-year-old daughter his offering envelope and told her to put it in the plate. She asked what it was for, and he told her it was for Jesus.

After the usher had collected her envelope, she whispered, "That's not Jesus; that's Sophie's Dad!"

SMILEY ANDERS
BATON ROUGE (LOUISIANA) *ADVOCATE*

Good Steward

A little boy came home eating a candy bar. His mother asked him where he got it.

"I bought it at the store with the dollar you gave me," he said.

"But that dollar was for Sunday school," his mother replied.

"I know, Mom, but the pastor met me at the door and got me in for free," the boy said.

NORMA SIMS
EUSTIS, FLORIDA

Like Any Parents

Our confirmation class for middle school children talked one day about Jesus being in the temple "about My Father's business." We talked about how worried Mary and Joseph must have been when they noticed Him missing after three days.

The teacher asked the students what they thought Mary might have said to Jesus after they found Him.

One of the kids answered: "Get Your butt into the car!"

MARIAN ELY
RENTON, WASHINGTON

"Mom, I think I could skip my bath tonight
since I'm going to be baptized tomorrow."

from *JoyfulNoiseletter.com*
© Doc Goodwin.

Dunkin' Dollies

A woman took her four-year-old daughter to a baptismal service at her church. Later that night at home, her daughter took all her dolls into the bathtub with her and held her own baptismal service.

As she dunked each doll under the water, she repeated, "Now I baptize you in the name of the Father, the Son, and hold your nose."

SMILEY ANDERS
BATON ROUGE (LOUISIANA) *ADVOCATE*

Booo!

A six-year-old girl asked her grandmother: "Grandma, when you die, can you ask God one thing for me?"

"Sure, what do you want me to ask?" the grandmother replied.

"Ask Him, are dragons real?"

"How am I supposed to let you know what God says?" the grandmother asked.

"Just text me," the girl said. "Don't be a ghost. That would scare me."

JEFF TOTTEN

3

THE FAMILY CIRCUS
by Bil & Jeff Keane

**"Be quiet, Jeffy, or you'll be sent
to God's office."**

from *JoyfulNoiseletter.com*
© Bil Keane

"You Gotta Be Quiet in Church, or the 'Hushers' Will Get You!"

God's Kids in God's House

God's kids and God's house are most compatible. They sometimes provoke a look or two from fellow worshippers. Like when they get too exuberant in their praise, or when they feel compelled to pray, "Lead us not into temptation, but deliver us from e-mail," with a voice that causes worshippers three rows around to snap open their eyes and give out an unaccustomedly loud "Amen!" Or when little Emily needed a restroom—and very quickly. She jumped up and yelled, "Mommy, I gotta. . ." Fortunately the family reputation was saved when a well-trained hand covered a much-too-expressive mouth.

A Liturgical Sweep

A clergywoman and mother shared this story at a district United Methodist meeting in New Jersey.

The clergywoman was quickly vacuuming the living room floor of her home where her three-year-old child was playing. In a hurry, the mother approached the child, then said, "Lift up your feet!"

The child responded, "We lift them up to the Lord."

Rev. Donald DeGroat
Wanaque, New Jersey

Church Boxing

Pastor Gerald Krum of St. John's Lutheran Church, Lewistown, Pennsylvania, has a game plan for his children's sermons. A child brings up the box in which there is something the pastor has not seen. Krum must create a message on what he finds in the box.

One Sunday morning, Patrick presented the pastor with a box with a portable phone inside.

"We have six members in the hospital now," the pastor began. "I think I'll call God and ask Him to help them get better. Now what is His number? I'll try 555-2156." After he dialed the number, he said, "No, that's not it. What should I dial next?"

"Try 911," little Alex answered.

Pastoral Prayer

From the pulpit the pastor declared, "Lord, without You we are but dust."

A four-year-old girl leaned over and asked her mother in a loud voice, "Mommy, what is butt dust?"

JEFF TOTTEN

Pepperoni in Advent

During the children's sermon on the third Sunday in Advent at First Baptist Church in Gainesville, Florida, the youth minister remarked: "Bethlehem was a real small town. In fact, it was so small, I'll bet they didn't even have a Pizza Hut."

One young lad quickly and seriously remarked: "Maybe they had a Little Caesars!"

PASTOR LYNWOOD WALTERS
GAINESVILLE, FLORIDA

Stop and Go

A mother took her small son to a Catholic church one Sunday morning. As the mass went on and on, he became restless. She tried, in vain, to assure the little boy that the mass would soon be over. Finally, he pointed to the tabernacle votive light—a candle in a red glass container that always stays lit—and asked: "Are we going to have to stay here until that red light turns green?"

FR. NORMAN MUCKERMAN
LIGUORI, MISSOURI

Direction, Please

In fifty years as a pastor, the only time I ever laughed during the invitation was when eight-year-old Andy came down the aisle. Andy had been in Sunday school and vacation Bible school almost from birth, but had never made a profession of faith.

Recently, at an invitation, when Andy came down the aisle, I rejoiced and thanked God that, finally, Andy had come forward. I bent down and said, "God bless you, Andy. Do you want to accept Christ and be baptized?"

He replied, "No, I want to go to the bathroom."

I burst out laughing and so did the entire congregation.

PASTOR JOHN T. JAMES
SARASOTA, FLORIDA

"Your quarter rolled under the seat, Mister."

The Naked Truth

Pastor Stan Holdeman of Garden Baptist Church, Indianapolis, Indiana, went to an informal church gathering wearing shorts and a T-shirt. A little girl from a newly churched family who had seen him only in his Sunday morning suits loudly proclaimed: "Hey, preacher, you sure look different with clothes on!"

For All Aarons

In his first pastorate in Northfield, Vermont, Rev. Gordon T. Wells of Worcester, Vermont, had in his congregation an adorable two-year-old boy named Aaron. Without fail toward the end of Rev. Well's sermons, Aaron would say to his father, "Done, Daddy, done?"

The congregation would chuckle, and the parents would *sssh* him. Rev. Wells endured the interruptions with patient good humor, and he says, "In order to hold my congregation's attention until the end, I began concluding every sermon in the same way with the remark, 'Done, Aaron, done.'"

No Repeats, Please!

After a worship service at First Baptist Church in New Castle, Kentucky, a mother with a fidgety seven-year-old boy told Pastor Dave Charlton how she finally got her son to sit still and be quiet. About halfway through the sermon, she leaned over and whispered: "If you don't be quiet, Pastor Charlton is going to lose his place and will have to start his sermon all over again!" It worked.

PASTOR DAVE CHARLTON
NEW CASTLE, KENTUCKY

Newsworthy

When my son Michael was three years old, I took him to church one Sunday, and we sat in a pew close to the front. This particular Sunday our paperboy was the altar boy.

When the mass was about to begin, the priest and the altar boy came out on the altar. Michael stood up in the pew, pointed, and yelled loud and clear: "Look, Mommy, there's God and the paperboy."

LAURETTA LEPINSKI
BUFFALO, MINNESOTA

So There!

At church one Sunday morning, the small son of the Baptist pastor watched with wide eyes the baptism by immersion of a churchgoer. He was fascinated because he had never seen a baptism.

The boy decided to baptize his cat in the bathtub. The cat struggled mightily to get out of the water, spit, and clawed at the boy. Finally, the cat jumped out of the bathtub and escaped.

"Okay," the boy sighed, "be a Methodist!"

CURTIS ANDERSON
FORT WORTH, TEXAS

Water Proof

Three children were to be christened at St. Aloysius Catholic Church. Two were infants, but the third was a two-year-old boy who wanted no part of the ceremony.

So to convince the boy that it wasn't a painful experience, Rev. Donald Blanchard sprinkled his dad with holy water—then proceeded to douse himself.

After that, the youngster couldn't wait to get his hair wet, and submitted cheerfully.

JEFF TOTTEN

Denominationalism

Pastor Bob Thompson of Corinth Reformed Church in Hickory, North Carolina, reports that each year the church's confirmands are required to visit another church and write a brief essay on their experiences—and how the experience affected them.

Here are some of Thompson's favorite responses from this year's essays:

- Baptist church: "During one part of the service in the background they had a Baptist pool. We had a chance to see some get dipped into the pool full body."

- Catholic church: "They also did all these strange hand signals that I didn't know."

- African American church: "They only beat us in one thing: staying on beat."

- Methodist church: "Another thing I noticed was that the assistant pastor dozed off during the other pastor's sermon."

- Pentecostal church: "During the sermon the pastor would randomly start crying. He cried a lot."

- "The church I visited was called First Methodist which is a Baptist church."

4

THE FAMILY CIRCUS
by Bil & Jeff Keane

**"Why doesn't THAT organist ever play
'Take Me Out to the Ball Game'?"**

from *JoyfulNoiseletter.com*
© Bil Keane.

"How Come?"

God's Kids Want to Know

It must be universal, the number of times a kid can ask "Why?" and "How?" or the variation, "How come?" These questions ring in their parents', teachers', and church leaders' ears.

Why? It's just because kids want to know.

Only Way?

For many years, a pastor had a reputation for his excellent sermons, which were not only inspiring but usually short. Interviewed by a newspaper reporter, the pastor explained that, as a young man, he learned the importance of being brief and to the point.

"One Sunday I was delivering a sermon to my first congregation," he said, "and I became carried away with the sound of my own words, and didn't realize how restless people were becoming.

"Then a small boy, who had been squirming and fidgeting in the front pew, caught my attention. I saw him tug at his mother's sleeve and then, in a voice that could be heard throughout the church, he said, 'Mommy, are you sure this is the only way to get to heaven?'"

JIM REED
COTTER, ARKANSAS

A Question of Water

One of my relatives had a precocious child and chose not to have him baptized until he was three. Joe was very much into what was happening during the initial part of the Methodist ceremony.

All went well until the water was put on his head, when he hollered out for the entire congregation to hear, "Don't you know you're getting my head wet?"

DOTTIE KENNEDY
DEARBORN, MICHIGAN

Daddy Knows

R. Alan Stewart, DDS, passed this one on from Grandma Gail:

A weary mother of four-year-old triplet boys went upstairs for the third time to settle them down for their bedtime. This time she raised her voice.

One of the boys said, "Mommy, God doesn't like it when we yell."

His brother turned to him and said, "Do you think Daddy knows that?"

Saints versus Saints

During a dismal season of losses by the New Orleans Saints football team, a mother mentioned to her five-year-old daughter that the family was going to attend mass in celebration of All Saints Day.

The little girl replied, "Why? Did they win a game?"

JEFF TOTTEN

Lettuce Pray?

On the way to school one morning, three-year-old Emma asked her mother if God's wife was named "Lettuce."

The mother replied that she did not think God had a wife, and if He did, she doubted that He would call her Lettuce.

The little girl answered: "Then who are we praying to in church when the man says 'Lettuce pray'?"

A Guy Needs to Know

A teenager's question in a Sunday school class: "When you die and go to heaven, do you get stuck wearing the clothes you were buried in for eternity?"

GEORGE GOLDTRAP

Makes Sense

Three-year-old Rowan was struggling over my name. His grandmother reminded him, "This is Pastor Tina."

Rowan said, "Hello, Mrs. Pastor Tina," and then, asking about my husband, added, "and how is Mr. Pastor Tina?"

PASTOR TINA BANFILL
ORLAND, CALIFORNIA

Kids' Questions for God

"Dear God: My Sunday school teacher said You are a jealous God. I thought You had everything You wanted."

JOHN, AGE 9

"Dear God: Is Rev. Lambert a friend of Yours, or do You just know Him through the business?"

MARTHA, AGE 8

"Is it true my father won't get in heaven if he uses his golf words in the house?"

LUCILLE, AGE 8

"Dear God: In school we read that Thomas Edison made light, but in Sunday school they said You did it first. Did he steal Your idea?"

MARK, AGE 8

"Dear God: I keep waiting for spring, but it never did come yet. What's up? Don't forget."

DAVID, AGE 7

"Dear God: In school they told us what You do. Who does it when You are on vacation?"

JAMES, AGE 7

DOTTIE SOGOIAN
LIVONIA, MICHIGAN

More Questions

"Dear God: I'd like to live for 900 years like that guy in the Bible. See what You can do for me, please."

JIM, AGE 6

"Dear God: My Grandpa says You were around when he was a little boy. How far back do You go?"

DONALD, AGE 8

"Dear God: Do You really mean, do unto others as they do unto you? If You did, then I'm going to get even with my brother."

ALLISON, AGE 7

"Dear God: It's great the way You always get the stars in the right place at night. Why can't You do that with the moon?"

KATE, AGE 6

Glad You Asked

When my father passed away, the family was greeting people at the viewing. My cousin brought along her twin granddaughters, both in kindergarten.

The twins shyly approached my mother and asked, "Aunt Dorothy, could we ask you a question?"

Knowing that this was the first death that the twins had experienced, my mother braced herself for a question on mortality; then she noticed that they were staring at her hair. It was my mother's custom to twist her waist-length hair and comb it up to form a bun on top of her head.

The twins asked, "We want to know why everybody else's hair grows down, but yours grows up."

In the many days of mourning that followed, my mother would laugh again and again when remembering the twin's question.

BRIAN HICE
MARSHALL, MICHIGAN

"You're the theology expert around here. . . .
Can we baptize Beanie Babies?"

from *JoyfulNoiseletter.com*
© Jonny Hawkins.

Tell Me

Our three-year-old son, Thomas Jesse, has just started Sunday school. We have been talking about the Ten Commandments and trying to reinforce them. When he asks why he has to do or not do something, I usually tell him, "Because Jesus says so, and we need to do as He says."

Recently, he was in a car riding with his grandma. He asked her to drive faster. His grandma explained to him that the sign said she could only drive thirty miles per hour.

He then asked her, "Did Jesus say that?"

CATHY MEADOWS
CONNORSVILLE, INDIANA

Sacramental Use Only

At an infant baptism, while the pastor was pouring water over the head of the baby, a little girl in the congregation whispered to her mother: "Mom, is that how they brainwash babies?"

PASTOR DICK DINGES
VIRGINIA BEACH, VIRGINIA

Woops!

A little girl noticed that her mother's brown hair had a few strands of white hair. "Mom, why are some of your hairs white?" she asked.

"Well," her mother answered, "every time you do something wrong and make me unhappy, one of my hairs turns white."

The little girl pondered the answer, then asked, "Mom, why are *all* of Grandma's hairs white?"

GEORGE GOLDTRAP

WC Etiquette

The second grader came up to Sister Sharon's desk and said, "I have to go to the bathroom."

Sister corrected him in a whisper, "*May* I go to the bathroom?"

"Do you have to go, too?" he asked.

A Family Thing

Our daughter Dani Dee is four years old. Her Grandpa Matt died before she was born, so we frequently talk about her grandpa in heaven.

One night at bedtime, we found Dani Dee out on the deck in her pajamas with her arms reaching out toward the sky. She was yelling, "God, can You hear me? Please let Grandpa Matt come down from heaven."

She paused and then said, "Okay, how about You, Jesus. Can You hear me?"

Jo Anna Tacheny
Burnsville, Minnesota

Mommy Knows Best

After a storm, Leola R. Goit of Brookings, Oregon, took her son, Gary, then three, for a walk along a beach on the Pacific Ocean. The path was covered with foam.

The boy pointed to the foam and asked, "How much soap did God put in the ocean, Mommy?"

The 100-Gun Salute

During the opening ceremonies of the Missouri State Fair, the governor was honored with a nineteen-gun salute. The emcee explained that a twenty-one-gun salute would mean that the president was in attendance.

My eight-year-old son, Brady, asked me what it would mean if it had been a 100-gun salute. I said I didn't know.

"Well," he said, "I bet it means that God is in town."

TERRI CUNNINGHAM
SEDALIA, MISSOURI

Literal Translation

After Bishop Emeritus Kenneth Povish of Lansing, Michigan, instituted at his parish a weekly litany of divine praises of God for the holiness of the saints, a young mother attended with her son, a third grader. After church, the boy asked his mother: "What's a spouse?"

"A spouse is somebody's husband or wife," the mother replied. "Why do you ask?"

"What does 'most chaste spouse' mean?" the boy asked.

"That means St. Joseph was a good, pure, and holy husband," the mother answered. "What do you think 'most chaste spouse' means?"

Rather reluctantly the boy finally replied, "Well, I think it means that all the women were after him, but Mary got him in the end."

HARRIET ADAMS
MORTON, PENNSYLVANIA

Just in Case

My husband was putting our five-year-old son, Zach, to bed when Zach asked, "Dad are you afraid of anything?"

My husband replied, "Well, when I was a little boy, when the lights were off, sometimes I was a little afraid of the dark."

Zach said, "I'm not afraid, Daddy, because God is with me all the time." He paused and pulled a flashlight from under the covers. "And besides—I have a flashlight!"

JILL HOWELL
WILMINGTON, NORTH CAROLINA

The Best Policy

At a church service, Rev. Gary Blume, minister of First Church in Weymouth, Massachusetts, was telling a children's story to illustrate "honesty." Suddenly, his three-year-old son, Gregory, stood up and in a loud voice asked, "Hey, Dad, is that really true, or are you just preaching?"

REV. HARRY MAHONEY
DEDHAM, MASSACHUSETTS

A Twin Tale

Richard B. Butler of Fredericksburg, Texas, and his wife were sitting in church before the start of the morning service when two little girls, about three years old, sat with their mother in front of the Butlers. They appeared to be identical twins.

Butler leaned forward and asked them, "Are you girls twins?"

"Yes!" one of the girls replied, "Mother, how long have we been twins?"

Ape Logic

A six-year-old boy was taken by his mother to the zoo. They saw a gorilla sitting on a tree stump. On the ground to the gorilla's left was one book, the Bible; on his right was another book.

The gorilla would alternately pick up one book and thumb through the pages, then pick up the other book and thumb through the pages.

"What is he doing, Mommy?" the boy asked.

"I don't know," the mother replied. "Let's ask the zookeeper."

The zookeeper explained the bizarre behavior as follows:

"On the gorilla's right is Darwin's *Theory of Evolution*. He's trying to figure out whether he's his keeper's brother or his brother's keeper."

DON COOPER, MD
STILLWATER, OKLAHOMA

Address, Please

During a flight, flight attendant Lynette Robinson of Elk River, Minnesota, was called over to a little girl's seat. The youngster, looking searchingly out of the plane window, turned to the flight attendant and asked: "Which cloud does God live in?"

JEFF TOTTEN

No Returns Allowed

A little boy's new baby brother wouldn't stop crying and screaming.

"Where did we get him?" he asked his mother.

"He came from heaven, dear," the mother replied.

"I can see why they threw him out!" the boy exclaimed.

LOIS WARD
LONGMONT, COLORADO

Or Maybe Superman

I was helping with child care one Sunday morning. With me was a young boy whose family did not attend church. The pastor often popped into the child-care room before worship to say hello to the children.

That morning he was rushed and came flying into the room with his black robe unzipped and billowing out behind him. After he left, Derek looked up at me and whispered, "Who was that? Batman?"

PASTOR SANDI REHE
WILLIAMSTOWN, MASSACHUSETTS

Something like That

Dr. Ron Lavin of Encinitas, California, author of a new book entitled *Turning Griping into Gratitude* (CSS Publishers) passed on this story:

When I was the pastor of Our Savior's Lutheran Church in Tucson, Arizona, the parents of a four-year-old girl named Beth brought her to church on the Saturday before her baptism. The girl looked frightened. I tried everything I could think of to help the little girl feel comfortable with what was going to happen at her baptism the next day.

I told her she that she was getting God as her Father, that God loved her and wanted her in His family. Nothing seemed to work.

The next morning at church, the mother told me: "I explained it again to Beth last night. This morning she came skipping down the hall and ran into our bedroom with a happy face. She asked, 'Is this the day I get pasteurized?'"

Mass Ed

Fr. John Hissrich of Guardian Angels Catholic Parish in Pittsburgh, Pennsylvania, was teaching a fifth-grade class about some of the things that are done at mass. He told them that incense is sometimes used at the reading of the Gospel, and that they may see the altar server come out carrying incense.

One boy, with a rather squeamish look on his face, raised his hand and asked, "Father, are the insects alive?"

Well, Why Not?

After Sunday school, a mother told her small daughter that the Bible says Jesus will return to the earth someday.

"When is He coming back?" the daughter asked.

"I don't know," the mother replied.

"Can't you look it up on the Internet?" the girl asked.

JEFF TOTTEN

Just Click It

A three-year-old boy watched the weather go from rainy to sunny to rainy and sunny again within minutes.

"Grandma," he asked, "does God have a remote control?"

JOAN N. HARRIS
SILER CITY, NORTH CAROLINA
COUNTRY WOMAN MAGAZINE

Good Question

A mother brought home a new grill she'd purchased. Her seven-year-old son asked her what it was. She told him it was a George Foreman grill.

"George Washington?" he asked.

"No, George Foreman. He's a boxer and a Christian," she replied.

"How can he be a dog and be a Christian?" he asked.

JOANNE PHARIS
FORT WORTH STAR TELEGRAM

There He Is

After church, a little girl turned to her mother and asked, "The pastor said that God is bigger than we are, and God lives within us. Is that true?"

"Yes," her mother replied.

"Well," the girl said, "if God is bigger than us and He lives in us, wouldn't He show through?"

LOIS WARD

How Come?

A young boy asked his mother, a pastor, why she prayed before she preached. His mother replied, "I ask God to help me preach a better sermon."

"Well then, why doesn't God help you?" the boy said.

REV. CHRIS ANDERSON
YORK, PENNSYLVANIA

A Fiscal Issue

Dr. Cliff Houston, pastor of Pittsford, New York, Baptist Church, was invited to be the visiting preacher at First United Methodist Church in Blakely, Georgia, when he visited his hometown recently. He began his sermon with this story:

"Our church in Pittsford recently began having the offertory after the sermon, just at the close of the service. On one of the first Sundays after this change, I overheard a child in the congregation tell her mother, 'Doesn't he know we haven't paid him yet?'"

CHARLES GARRETT
FORT GAINES, FLORIDA

Family Species

After Sunday school, a little boy said to his mother, "You told me we were created by God, but Dad said we are descended from monkeys. Who is right?"

"Well," the boy's mom replied, "your father is just talking about his side of the family."

BRUCE JOHNSON
KALAMAZOO, MICHIGAN

5

THE FAMILY CIRCUS
by Bil & Jeff Keane

"I'm a REAL superhero. I'm Daddy."

from *JoyfulNoiseletter.com*
© Bil Keane.

"Why Did Pastor Just Call Daddy 'Brother'?"

God's Kids in the Family Circle

There was a time in some churches when the members called each other "brother" and "sister." Lots of kids grew up thinking they were part of the biggest family in the whole wide world. As a matter of fact—they were—and are!

Lost and Found

On a recent Sunday at Lititz, Pennsylvania, Moravian Church, I was talking with the children in the "Children's Chat" in worship about Luke 15 (the lost sheep and the lost coin), and the joy we feel when we find something valued that we lost.

I asked the children if they ever lost something and then found it. Young Jordan said, "Yeah, I lost a five-dollar bill once, and I found it in my brother Cody's wallet."

Older brother Cody was also there, and didn't appreciate it, but the congregation took a long time to stop laughing.

REV. DEAN JURGEN
LITITZ, PENNSYLVANIA

Lecture on Thanks

Tina, a middle school teacher, tried to explain Thanksgiving to her four-year-old nephew, who thought it was a boring holiday with no presents or treats. She patiently explained that it was a time for appreciating all we have: a loving family, health, good food, etc.

At bedtime on Thanksgiving evening, Tina

overheard the boy saying this prayer:

"Dear God: I am thankful for Mommy and Daddy and my sister—even though she breaks my toys—and my food and my warm house and my toys. I am thankful for my Aunt Tina, but could You tell her that she talks too much! I am only four!"

Smiley Anders
Baton Rouge (Louisiana) *Advocate*

What's That You Say?

Visiting their grandmother's house at Christmastime, two young boys were saying their prayers at bedtime. The younger boy started loudly shouting his prayers: "God, please send me a Nintendo...and a new bike...!"

"Why are you shouting your prayers?" his older brother asked. "God isn't deaf."

"No, but grandma almost is!" his little brother answered.

Thomas G. Bassett
Syracuse, New York

Chance of Showers

After a four-year-old girl's grandfather passed away, every time it would rain, she would go to the window, pull the curtains closed, and exclaim, "Nobody look up in the sky! Grandpa's taking a shower!"

JANET BEHNING
MESQUITE, TEXAS

Not Quite the Same

After hearing their pastor preach about the devil, before Halloween, two boys were walking home from church. "What do you think about all that stuff about the devil?" one boy asked the other.

Replied the other boy, "Yeah, you know how Santa Claus turned out. It's probably just your dad."

BUD FRIMOTH
PORTLAND, OREGON

"WOWWW! Say a prayer that we can stay up here forever, Mom!"

Our Father and Mommy

Lauri Rodrigue of Thibodaux, Louisiana, was trying to teach her two-year-old twins, Tricia Lynn and Reese Amanda, to recite the Lord's Prayer.

She was having difficulty because each time she would begin, "Our Father. . ." the twins would always add, ". . .and my mommy."

A Real Bell Ringer

Rev. James L. Garner Jr., pastor of the First United Methodist Church of Millersville, Pennsylvania, happened upon his two young sons taunting and arguing with each other.

"Oh, yeah?" said the older.

"Yeah!" replied the younger.

"You and what army?" exclaimed the older.

"The Salvation Army," replied the younger.

Coulda Fooled Me

When asked her name, a little girl would reply "I'm Mr. Maddox's daughter." Her mother told her this was wrong, that she should say, "I'm Martha Maddox."

In church one Sunday morning, the pastor said to her, "Aren't you Mr. Maddox's daughter?"

The girl replied, "I thought I was, but my mother says I'm not."

REV. JIM KENNEY
MISSION, KANSAS

9/11–Hike!

Shortly after the calamitous events of September 11, 2001, Bob Stoops, coach of the University of Oklahoma football team, was listening to the bedtime prayers of his two two-year-old twin sons, Drake and Isaac. One boy concluded his prayer with, "And, dear God, please bless Coach Bush," and the other boy responded, "Yeah."

DR. DON AND DONNA COOPER
STILLWATER, OKLAHOMA

Now Hear This

A little boy had to go to the bathroom during the church service, so his father took him. When they returned to their pew, the child turned to people in the pew behind him and said, "You know what? My daddy went potty, too."

REV. KARL R. KRAFT

My Mother

A group of elementary school children was asked why God made mothers.

"To help us out there when we were getting born," one child replied.

"She's the only one who knows where the Scotch tape is," a second child answered.

Asked what ingredients mothers are made of, another child replied, "God makes mothers out of clouds and angel hair and everything nice in the world and one dab of mean."

The children also were asked, "Why did God give you your mother and not some other mom?"

"God knew she likes me a lot more than other people's moms like me," replied a little boy.

"Because we're related," a little girl said.

Asked what the difference is between moms

and dads, one child said, "Moms have magic. They make you feel better without medicine."

The children were asked, "If you could change one thing about your mom, what would it be?"

"I would like for her to get rid of those invisible eyes in the back of her head," one child replied.

Said another, "She has this weird thing about keeping my room clean. I'd get rid of that."

Still another child replied, "I'd make my mom smarter. Then she would know my sister did it, not me."

GEORGE GOLDTRAP

Grandma's Fun

At the funeral of a grandmother, family members were asked to place something of sentimental value inside the casket. A little girl wrote this note for the casket: "Dear Grandma, I hope you're having a lot of fun in heaven with God."

PASTOR DICK DINGES

Tough Love

A little girl wrote to God: "Dear God, is it hard to love everybody in the whole world? There are only five people in my family, and it's hard to always love them."

LILLI VORSE
COUNCIL BLUFFS, IOWA

Family Trait

When I began my sermon one Sunday, it became obvious that my young son was fidgety. His mother whispered to him, "Please be quiet. You are not supposed to talk during church."

He immediately stood in the pew, pointed directly at me, and declared in a loud voice, "Well, Daddy is talking!"

REV. ROBERT R. ALLEN
OXFORD, MISSISSIPPI

Who's the Light?

A mother had carefully coached her small daughter who was to appear in a children's play in a Reformed church. The girl's only lines were: "I am the light of the world." But she forgot her lines.

Her mother came forward and whispered in her ear: "I am the light of the world."

"My mom is the light of the world!" the girl exclaimed.

Real Communion

LTC Drusilla B. Grubb, of Stuttgart, Germany, witnessed this scene on a playground:

"My son, then two, had spilled his Coke and my daughter, then four, was sharing by giving him sips from her Coke can. I thought there was an air of importance in her gestures and edged closer to listen in. As she gave him sips from her Coke, I overheard her say: 'The Coke of Christ; the soda of salvation.'"

Country Blues

Country singer Barbara Mandrell said that when her son Nathan was young, she always sang three songs to him: "Jesus Loves Me," "This Is the Day the Lord Has Made," and "Jesus Loves the Little Children." She said: "I wondered which of these would be the first song that Nathan would sing on his own. It was none of those three. The first song he sang was 'All My Ex's Live in Texas.'"

THE DETROIT NEWS

Soccer Scores

Rev. Dave Fortuna of Lea Joyner Memorial United Methodist Church, Monroe, Louisiana:

Competition is everywhere and in single portions is healthy, but in many cases it's overemphasized and leads to the fatal attitude that "winning is everything." My five-year-old nephew, David, gave me a sermon illustration that keeps things in perspective.

After David played in a soccer game, his father asked him, "Hey, David, did you win?"

"I think so," the boy said.

"Well, what was the score, son?" his father asked.

"Six!" the boy replied.

"Every Good Boy Does Fine"

A mother told her young son to go to bed and be sure to say his prayers and ask God to make him a good boy. The boy's father, passing by the bedroom, overheard his son praying: "And, God, make me a good boy if You can; and if You can't, don't worry about it, 'cause I'm having fun the way I am."

MSGR. ARTHUR TONNE
JOKES PRIESTS CAN TELL

Kid's Boss

Our son, Kevin, is a typical two-year-old; he likes to say "no" when he is told to do something. One day after the fifth "no" from Kevin, I decided to reason with him. I wanted him to realize that I was the authority figure in our home, and he had to obey me.

I asked, "Kevin, who is the daddy here?"

He pointed at me.

"And who is the boy here?" I asked.

He pointed at himself.

"And who is in charge here?" I asked.

Kevin thought for a moment and said, "Mommy."

DANIEL HINTZ
GRAND ISLAND, NEBRASKA

THE FAMILY CIRCUS
by Bil & Jeff Keane

"I figured out a system for getting along with my mom. She tells me what to do and I do it."

from *JoyfulNoiseletter.com*
© Bil Keane.

She's Always Been Mom

A Sunday school teacher asked her youngsters, "What kind of a little girl was your mom?"

A boy replied, "I don't know because I wasn't there, but my guess would be she was pretty bossy."

A girl answered, "They say she used to be nice."

Another girl replied, "My mom has always been my mom and none of that other stuff."

NORMA SIMS

Sermon Wise

One Sunday morning, I was sitting in church right behind the pastor's spouse and their two children. When the pastor entered the pulpit to preach, the seven-year-old son asked his mother if he could go to the nursery.

His mother replied: "No, you're too old to go to the nursery."

The pastor's son protested loudly, "But Mom, I heard it last night and it's a long one."

REV. VIRGINIA K. BARNES
JACKSONVILLE, FLORIDA

Varoom, Varoom!

Our church service and Sunday school classes are both held from 10:00 to 11:00 a.m. One Sunday, the six-year-olds were dismissed early and headed for the lobby to wait for their parents.

Suddenly, the minister's son raced through the lobby and down the aisle, behind the wheel of an imaginary race car, providing his own sound effects at the top of his lungs. *"Varooooom! Screeeeech!"* he cried, as he leaned into a hairpin turn into the front-row pew and sat down next to his embarrassed mother.

Unshaken, his father interrupted his sermon just long enough to say, "Park it, Philip, and give the keys to your mother."

PAT HADSELL
FORT WORTH (TEXAS) *STAR-TELEGRAM*

Pip of a Pope

An eight-year-old boy was getting a rare treat. He was invited to visit the sacristy where the priests donned vestments for mass. The priest would explain each vestment. When they arrived, the priest asked the boy his name.

"John Paul," the boy replied.

"Oh, the same name as the pope," the priest said.

"Yes." The little guy beamed. "But my parents call me the 'Pip.'"

BOBBE LYON
MAITLAND, FLORIDA

A Sincere Prayer

A Sunday school teacher said to a little boy in her class: "So your mother says your prayers for you every night at bedtime? That's very nice. What does she say?"

"Thank God he's in bed!" the little boy replied.

Grandparents' Sunday

A little girl sat on her grandfather's lap as he read her a bedtime story. From time to time, she'd reach up and touch his wrinkled cheek. Then she'd touch her own cheek thoughtfully.

Finally she spoke, "Grandpa, did God make you?"

"Yes, sweetheart," he answered. "God made me a long time ago."

"Did God make me, too?" she asked.

"Yes indeed, honey," he answered. "God made you just a little while ago."

She touched his cheek again, and then her own.

"Well, He's doing better work today, isn't He?"

BART VAN GIESSEN
TEXAS TOWNSHIP, MICHIGAN

6

"Don't get mixed up and marry me to him!"

from *JoyfulNoiseletter.com*
© Goddard Sherman.

"Sure I Know the Difference; Girls Are Pink and Boys Are Blue"

God's Kids and the Birds and Bees

The parents' dreaded question: "Hey, Mom, where did I come from?" which often results in an age-appropriate description of reproduction, and sweaty palms. Followed by total silence, until Junior announces, "Oh yeah? Tommy says he came from Los Angeles." Nonetheless, there are always kid funnies, even in this ticklish subject.

A Fine Proposal

One of Sister Myra's preschoolers announced, "When I grow up, I'm going to marry you."

Showing the children the plain silver band on her ring finger, sister said, "Your mother has a wedding ring like this. What does that mean?"

"That she belongs to my dad," the little boy answered.

"My ring means that I belong to God," sister explained.

Undaunted, the boy replied, "Well, I'd get you one with a stone."

Infant Economics

After her mother gave birth to twin boys, a pastor saw the five-year-old sister of the two boys at the hospital.

"I hear God has sent you two more little brothers, Diane," the pastor said cheerfully.

"Yes, sir," the little girl replied, "and He knows where the money's coming from. I heard Daddy say so."

A Little Girl's View

Asked, "How do you decide who to marry?" an eleven-year-old girl wrote:

"No person really decides before they grow up who they're going to marry. God decides it all way before, and you get to find out later who you're stuck with."

NEWSLETTER OF UNION PARK UMC
DES MOINES, IOWA

Love Is. . .

"Love is what makes you smile when you're tired."

FIVE-YEAR-OLD GIRL

"Love is when your puppy licks your face even after you left him alone all day."

FOUR-YEAR-OLD BOY

"Love is when a girl puts on a perfume and a boy puts on shaving cologne and they go out and smell each other."

FIVE-YEAR-OLD BOY

JODY DAVIS
INDIANAPOLIS, INDIANA

I'll Take Two

A four-year-old boy who had been adopted was told by his new parents that "Jesus gave you to us." The parents also refer to church as "Jesus' house," and he therefore believes that the priest, Fr. Shelton Fabré, is "Jesus."

The boy had seen Fr. Shelton walk up and down the aisle presenting newly baptized babies to the congregation at past masses.

One Sunday, the boy asked his grandmother, "Grammy, is Jesus gonna hand out babies today?"

SMILEY ANDERS
BATON ROUGE (LOUISIANA) *ADVOCATE*

Please

Two small children—a brother and a sister—entered the following prayer request in the Intercessory Prayer Book of the Mantua, New Jersey, United Methodist Church:

"My cat Scrapper. If she doesn't get out of heat we can't keep her."

REV. KARL R. KRAFT

Food Facts

My five-year-old daughter and three-year-old son were watching the Christmas story on TV as I prepared dinner. I heard my son ask his sister, "What is a virgin?"

As my mind raced to think of what to say, she answered for me: "It's a lady who eats all her vegetables."

DIANE CARLSON

Natal Tale

The nun read to her first-grade class the story of the birth of Jesus. "What do we learn from this story?" she asked.

Up went Jimmy's hand. He declared loudly: "This story tells us that we don't have to go to a hospital to get a baby."

MSGR. ARTHUR TONNE
JOKES PRIESTS CAN TELL

One of Each

Joe Garagiola, who donates time to St. Peter's Indian Mission School in Bapchule, Arizona, heard this story from Sr. Thereselle at the school:

Sr. Thereselle was reviewing the story of Noah's ark with her second-grade class. She asked, "Who was on the ark with Noah?"

A little girl replied, "Two animals of every kind."

"Why two?" sister asked.

"Well, there was a female and a. . ." the little girl thought hard. "a female and an e-mail!"

GINA BRIDGEMAN
SCOTTSDALE, ARIZONA

From Norway

On Christmas Eve, a family followed their custom of gathering at Grandma's house. The children were playing with a nativity set.

Ten-year-old Joey pointed to seven-year-old Mary and told her, "She was the Virgin Mary. Are you a virgin, Mary?"

"I don't think so," Mary replied. "I think I'm Norwegian."

MINNEAPOLIS STAR TRIBUNE

My Daddy Says

Johnny: "My daddy says that love is a feeling you feel when you're about to feel a feeling you never felt before."

      Teacher: "What's that mean?"

      Johnny: "I dunno."

Egg on Her Face

During a discussion of creation, Darleen Anderson of Springfield, Missouri, asked her four-year-old grandson Shane: "Which came first, the chicken or the egg?"

"Oh Grandma, God was really first," Shane replied, and then added, "but were you second?"

SPRINGFIELD (MISSOURI) *NEWS-LEADER*

by Bil & Jeff Keane

"Can I be thankful without eatin' sweet pota-toes?"

"Yuck!" and Sometimes "Yum!"

God's Kids and Edibles

At one developmental stage kids will put anything in their mouths. Then something happens, they become selective and are able to lock their mouths shut so nary a leaf of spinach or a spoonful of oatmeal can get in. Makes one remember the old orange vegetable joke: "If carrots are so good for a kid's eyes, how come I see so many dead rabbits on the highway?"

Hospitality Inn

A little boy, playing the part of the innkeeper in the Christmas play, had only one line. He was to say to Joseph and Mary, "There is no room at the inn."

This line began to trouble the boy. He did not want to play the part of the callous person who had turned away the Christ child.

On the night of the performance, when Mary and Joseph knocked on the door of the inn, the little boy opened it and said, "There is no room at the inn." Then he quickly added, "But you can come in for a cup of hot coffee!"

REV. KERRY PRESNELL
CHILLICOTHE, MISSOURI

Naughty Girl's Psalm

A young girl, punished by her parents for misbehaving, was made to eat her dinner alone at a small table in the corner of the living room.

The rest of the family heard her praying over her meal: "I thank Thee, Lord, for preparing a table before me in the presence of mine enemies."

REV. KARL R. KRAFT

Chocolate Chip?

While I was putting away the china in our new home, I placed our two-year-old son, Grant, in his high chair and gave him a cookie. As I worked, he asked for a second cookie, and then a third.

When I said "No" to his request, he took his petition to a higher authority. I heard him praying, "Jesus, help me get a cookie." After a pause, he called out to me, "Jesus says yes! Jesus wants a cookie, too!"

GRACE ERICKSON
TORONTO, CANADA

I'll Take Strawberry

At the age of four, a little girl mostly dozed through her first Catholic mass. However, when the altar boy shook some bells during the consecration, the little girl sprang awake and hollered, "The ice cream man!"

JEFF TOTTEN

Something Fishy

The First United Methodist Church of Gilford, New Hampshire, has a children's story time shortly before the children leave for Sunday school. One Sunday after Easter, Rev. Victoria Wood Parrish told the children that after Jesus was resurrected, He saw his disciples fishing from the beach, helped them catch a net full of fish, and then shared a breakfast that Jesus had prepared for them.

When the pastor asked the children what they thought the disciples ate for breakfast, the youngest child answered: "Sushi!"

JOYCE KEYSER
GILFORD, NEW HAMPSHIRE

Granny Grace

A little boy and his family were having Thanksgiving dinner at his Grandma's house. The boy started eating right away.

"Tommy, wait until we say a prayer," his mother said. "We always say a prayer before we eat at our house."

"But this is Grandma's house," the boy replied, "and she knows how to cook."

JEFF TOTTEN

Wise Men

A three-year-old girl and her little cousin were playing with a nativity set. The girl moved the pieces around, identifying Mary and Joseph and the angels.

The she picked up the three robed wise men carrying their urns filled with gifts. "And then," she explained to her cousin, "came the ladies with the coffee!"

THE LUTHERAN

A Grace-Full Story

A woman took her five-year-old son into a restaurant for lunch. The boy asked to say grace. "God is good. God is great. Thank You for the food we eat, and I would even thank You more if Mom gets me ice cream for dessert. Amen."

Most of the nearby customers laughed, but the boy overheard a woman saying, "That's what's wrong with this country. Kids today don't even know how to pray. Can you imagine asking God for ice cream?"

The boy burst into tears. An elderly man nearby approached the table and told the boy, "I'm sure God thought that was a great prayer.

Too bad that woman never asked God for ice cream. Sometimes a little ice cream is good for the soul."

The mother ordered some ice cream for her son. But the boy picked up his ice cream and took it over to the woman's table and gave it to her.

"This is for you," he said, smiling. "Ice cream is good for the soul sometimes, and my soul is good already."

BUD FRIMOTH
PORTLAND, OREGON

Pass the Potato Salad

When my wife and I were missionaries, we dragged our children from church to church during furlough, and ate many potluck suppers at our supporting churches.

At one church, my wife, Linda, showed the children a stained-glass window of the Last Supper, and asked them what they thought it depicted. "Oh," our youngest answered, "that's Jesus at the potluck supper!"

REV. RICHARD WHITE
HAILEYBURG, ONTARIO

Flapjack Faith

Mom was making pancakes for breakfast, and five-year-old Timmy and four-year-old Billy were arguing over who should have the first one.

Mom saw this as an excellent opportunity to provide a lesson in sharing and said, "Wouldn't Jesus say, 'Let My brother have the first pancake?'"

Timmy turned to his little brother and said, "Billy, you be Jesus."

DOROTHY DERRIGAN-DELUYCK
KNOXVILLE, TENNESSEE

No Wolf He

During the children's sermon at the Church in Silver Lake, Ohio, Rev. Mary Willis was discussing Isaiah 11:6–9 with the children. "What would happen if the wolf were to lie down with the lamb?" she asked.

Sam Kittinger, age eight, responded, "I think he would be lamb chops."

TERRY HARSNEY
FAIRLAWN, OHIO

Grace

Our four-year-old grandson was learning his ABC's and how to say grace before meals. He got confused at one dinner. He bowed his head and said, "A. . .B. . .C. . ." Then he paused and said, "Wrong one" and proceeded with "God is great, God is good, let us thank Him for our food."

Max Franks
Savannah, Tennessee

A Cheesy Idea

A six-year-old girl was asked by her mother to get ready to go to church for the Christmas Eve service. The girl said she didn't want to go to church.

"It's Jesus' birthday party," her mother explained. "How would you like it if one of your friends didn't want to come to your birthday party?"

The girl replied, "Mom, just once I wish Jesus would have His birthday party at Chuck E. Cheese."

Jeff Totten

Weather or Not

When I was chaplain of Cardigan Mountain School in Canaan, New York, my student assistant one day was looking over the printed "grace list," preparing to lead the prayer just before our all-school meal. He asked whether he might use the prayer beginning with the words: "For sunshine at the window and fresh air at the door... we give Thee thanks, O Lord."

I suggested another grace might be more appropriate because of the forecast of rain. When the time for grace came, the boy stepped to the microphone and prayed: "For sunshine at the window with a 70 percent chance of rain..."

REV. HARRY MAHONEY
DEDHAM, MASSACHUSETTS

Potluck Faith

A teacher in a private school announced to her second-grade class that the next day's "show-and-tell" would focus on things that they frequently saw in their house of worship.

The next day, a little boy stood up and said, "My name is Daniel. I'm Jewish, and this is a Star of David."

A little girl stood up and said, "My name is Mary and I'm a Catholic. This is a crucifix."

Then another little boy stood up and said, "My name is Bobby. I'm a Methodist, and this is a casserole."

POLLY WALTHER
COMOLA, MICHIGAN

Go Italian

At an Easter Sunday mass in a Catholic church, a mother heard her five-year-old daughter singing joyfully in the pew, "Lasagna in the highest!"

JEFF TOTTEN

Palm Course

Attending Palm Sunday services with her parents, a little girl was given a palm branch, which she waved during the procession into the church. Everyone placed the palm branches at the altar. Returning to their pew, the little girl suddenly shouted, "Hey, I want my salad back!"

JEFF TOTTEN

Sharing

The night before Easter, our three-year-old son, Kyle, and I were making bunny cookies. After they had come out of the oven, he was in the family room enjoying a cookie and a glass of milk.

In a few minutes, he came out to the kitchen and said, "Guess what, Mom. I'm going to leave a bunny cookie for Jesus to eat."

JOYCE RAMSEY
FRIDLEY, MINNESOTA

Wonder Bread

At a Christmas Eve service, Rev. Larry Tingle, pastor of Mt. Olivet United Methodist Church in Arlington, Virginia, was able to worship with his family, including his young grandson, Jacob.

The family all received communion. After the service, Jacob ran back up to the altar, knelt down, looked back at his grandfather, and asked, "More bread, Pa?"

Rev. Tingle later commented: "Would that more of us would run to God and kneel, seeking more of what God has to offer."

REV. GEORGE STEWART
MONTVALE, VIRGINIA

GI Coffee

A small boy surprised his mom on Mother's Day by preparing breakfast and serving her in bed. The mother enjoyed the orange juice, cereal, and toast, and thanked her son.

But she didn't want to tell him that it was the worst cup of coffee she had ever had in her life. Forcing down the last sip, she noticed three green plastic army soldiers in the bottom of the cup.

"Honey," she asked, "why are there three plastic army soldiers in the bottom of my cup?"

"Well, Mom," the boy replied, "it's like on TV, 'The best part of waking up is soldiers in your cup.'"

REV. JOSEPH PHIPPS
ALLEGAN, MICHIGAN

Heavenly Calories

A fourth grader told Marilyn Hagerty, columnist for the *Grand Forks* (Minneosta) *Herald*: "Heaven is a place where you can eat and not get fat."

JEFF TOTTEN

Easter Eating

I was reading to my young daughter, Maria, a book about Holy Week and Easter, leaving out some words to see if she could read them. I was reading about Jesus' last night with the disciples, how He broke bread and shared it with them, then passed around the cup.

I read to her: "This was Jesus' last. . ."

"Snack!" she immediately answered.

GINA BRIDGEMAN

Tough Is, As. . .

My mother once cared for a neighbor's five-year-old boy for the day. The youngster had worn out my mother with his energy and endless questions. He asked what they were having for dinner. She said, "Chicken."

He replied, "I don't like chicken!"

Exasperated, she responded, "Tough!"

Later, when they sat down at suppertime, my mother asked the boy if he would say grace.

He prayed, "Dear God, thank You for the tough chicken. Amen."

LINDA SHEPARD
EVERETT, WASHINGTON

Wheeling Right Along

My sister, now retired, delivers hot meals to people for Meals on Wheels. She often takes her grandson, Kyle, along with her on these visits.

One day, on the way home, Kyle said, "Grandma, when you get old, I will bring meals to you. . .and when I get old you can bring meals to me."

REV. NORMAN KOHNS
CALEDONIA, MICHIGAN

The Other Kind of Meat

A young couple invited their pastor to their home for dinner. While they were in the kitchen, the pastor asked their small son what they were having for dinner.

"Goat," the little boy replied.

"Goat?" the pastor asked.

"Yeah," the boy said. "I heard Dad say to Mom, 'We might as well have the old goat over for dinner today.'"

REV. KARL R. KRAFT

Sailing Food

Lesla and Lloyd Anderson of Phoenix, Arizona, saw the following posted at Atonement Lutheran Church Preschool in Phoenix. It's a collection of thoughts about Noah's Ark from the three-year-old preschool classes.

☼ "It took long, long, long days to build the ark. It had a lot of stairs. They used wood from the forest. It took seven days to build. They had two side places for the animals. Bricks helped, too! They had grass and a flower place."

☼ "I think it took fifty days to build. They brought pudding, apples, pears, grapes, bananas, cheese, grass, carrots, seeds, olives, plums, peaches, hay, chocolate milk, water, and juice."

☼ "Noah's family played games together on the ark. They took naps with the animals. And they played fetch and ate peanuts."

☼ "It took four days to build the ark. Noah's family packed cereal, pancakes, waffles, bacon, eggs, rice, popsicles, chocolate, and spaghetti! Beans and milk, too."

☼ "Noah's family played hockey, soccer, and hide-and-seek with the animals! They also enjoyed fun with Play-Doh, blocks, and ABC games!"

☼ "Noah's family packed chicken nuggets, hay, dog food, hamburgers, watermelon, french fries, chocolate milk, and cookies on the ark! They played ring-around-the-rosy with the animals! Noah's family slept with the baby animals and fed them coconuts!"

JEFF TOTTEN

Table Grace

A Sunday school teacher asked the little boy: "Jimmy, let's be honest. Do you say your prayers before eating?"

"No, ma'am," Jimmy replied. "I don't have to. My mom is a good cook."

FR. TARAS MILES
BELFIELD, NORTH DAKOTA

On the Menu

A priest at St. Richard's Church in Jackson, Mississippi, was asking questions of children about to receive their first communion. "What was served at the Last Supper?" he asked a little girl.

The girl thought for a while, then replied, "Well, first they had a salad..."

JEFF TOTTEN

"Before they met Jesus, weren't the 12 disciples the Dirty Dozen?"

from *JoyfulNoiseletter.com*
© Jonny Hawkins.

"Was Jesus' Mother the Virgin Mary or the King James Virgin?"

God's Kids and Their Religious Education

Sometime in the distant past it was decided that kids ought to have Bible education tailored just for them. Little did those wise souls realize that such tutelage would be responsible for some of the funniest observations and responses that would provide teachers with stories to regale any

117

handy audience. Including thought-provoking questions like, "Was it Pontius the Pilot who helped Mary and Joseph and baby Jesus on their flight to Egypt?"

Do It Yourself

Our daughter, Jennifer, eleven, has never been a patient person. Everything has to be done right now. When she was five, she saw her older sister baptized, so she wanted to be baptized.

We tried to explain that she needed to be old enough to understand the commitment she was making to Christ. A few nights later, we heard violent splashing noises and spluttering coming from the bathroom.

I called out, "Jennifer, what are you doing?"

She replied with a shout, "I told Jesus I loved Him and baptized myself!"

REV. LARRY J. CROCKER
SAN ANTONIO, TEXAS

Where Art Thou?

A Sunday school teacher asked her class of small children, "What do we know about God?"

A five-year-old boy raised his hand and exclaimed, "God is an artist!"

"How do you know He's an artist?" the teacher asked.

"Because Jesus said, 'Our Father who does art in heaven. . .'!" the boy replied.

GEORGE GOLDTRAP

Well, Sure

In Sunday school, a small boy was asked to name the first man. "Adam," he replied.

"What was the name of the first woman?" the teacher asked.

The boy struggled with the question for some time, and finally said, "Madam."

Human Resources Department

A third-grade boy's view of God's jobs:

- One of God's main jobs is making people. He makes them to replace the ones that die, so there'll be enough people to take care of things on earth.

- He doesn't make grown-ups, just babies. I think because they are smaller and easier to make. He doesn't have time to take up His valuable time teaching them to talk and walk. He can just leave that up to mothers and fathers.

- God's second most important job is listening to prayers. An awful lot of this goes on, since some people, like preachers and things, pray at times besides bedtime.

- God doesn't have time to listen to radio or TV because of this. Because He hears everything, there must be a terrible lot of noise in His ears, unless He has thought of a way to turn it off.

- Atheists are people who don't believe in God. I don't think there are any in our town. At least there aren't any who come to our church.

ANN DANIEL
SANDUSKY, OHIO

"Sure God goes fishing, 'cause He comforts us with His rod and reel!"

from *JoyfulNoiseletter.com*
© Sandy Dean.

Excursion Time

In Sunday school, the teacher asked the second graders, "How many of you would like to go to heaven?"

All the children except Bobby raised their hands.

The teacher asked Bobby why he did not want to go to heaven.

"I'm sorry," the little boy replied, "but my mom told me to come right home after Sunday school."

Sorry

My four-year-old great-grandson, Jaxon Ayers, of Fort Worth, Texas, was taught in Sunday school that Jesus lives in his heart. Not long after, he fell and hit his chest on a rock.

He grabbed his chest and said, "Oh I hurt my chest!" Then, alarmed, he said, "Oh I hurt Jesus!"

EVELYN BRISCOE
OKMULGEE, OKLAHOMA

It's in the Bible

A pastor's wife caught three small boys stealing cherries from her cherry tree. "Do you know what the Bible says about thieves?" she upbraided them.

"Sure, ma'am," one boy replied. "'Today thou shalt be with me in paradise.'"

Q&A

Some answers given by Sunday school children to the following questions:

Question: How did God make mothers?
Answer: He used dirt, just like for the rest of us.

Question: What did mom need to know about dad before she married him?
Answer: She had to know his background. Like is he a crook? Does he get drunk on beer?

Question: Why did your mom marry your dad?
Answer: My grandma says that Mom didn't have her thinking cap on.

WINSLOW FOX, MD
CHELSEA, MICHIGAN

A Quieter Dad

A small boy told a Sunday school teacher: "When you die, God takes care of you like your parents did when you were alive—only God doesn't yell at you all the time."

REV. DENNIS R. FAKES
LINDSBORG, KANSAS

How True

In his book, *I Shall Not Want*, Robert Ketchum tells of a Sunday school teacher who asked her group of children if anyone could quote the entire twenty-third Psalm.

A four-year-old girl raised her hand. She came to the front of the room, faced the class, and said: "The Lord is my shepherd, that's all I want."

GEORGE GOLDTRAP

Without Pork

After Sunday school, Elsie Huber of Huntington, New York, asked her young son what he had learned. "In Him we live and move and have our beans," the boy replied.

Resurrection Exclamation!

Fr. Richard Carton, associate pastor of St. Catherine of Siena Church, Mountain Lakes, New Jersey, was speaking to a group of second graders about the Resurrection when one student asked, "What did Jesus say, right after He came out of the grave?"

It was a question of great theological importance, but Fr. Carton had to explain, in words suitable to his young audience, that the Gospels do not tell us just what He said.

The hand of one little girl shot up. "I know what He said, Father," she insisted.

"And what was that?" asked Fr. Carton.

"Ta-da!" the girl exclaimed.

ANDY FISHER
DENVILLE, NEW JERSEY

A Pampered Baby

In the kindergarten Sunday school class at Life Community Church in Sunnyvale, Texas, the teacher told the children that Jesus was just like any other baby. She said, "Mary fed Him, and rocked Him, and sang to Him, and bathed Him, and changed His diapers. . . ."

Every little mouth dropped open when the teacher said, "And changed His diapers." They all sat there speechless.

Finally, Bethany, my niece, told the teacher: "Don't you think that's kind of personal?"

JANET BEHNING
MESQUITE, TEXAS

"Hi-Ho, Hi-Ho"

The Sunday school teacher at our church, Sunrise Church in Rialto, California, was telling the little children in her class that God loves them all the time, even when they're grumpy.

"And Happy!" exclaimed Jeremy, my two-year-old grandson, adding, "And Sleepy and Dopey and Sneezy and Doc and Bashful."

CAROL A. REASONER
RIALTO, CALIFORNIA

The Sheepish Thief

Pastor Fred Sapp of the Lutheran Church of the Holy Trinity in Kailua-Kona, Hawaii, called the children up front on a recent Sunday morning, and talked to them about Jesus the Shepherd. Because the children in Hawaii don't know much about sheep, Sapp told them about sheep and herding and then asked if anyone knew what a shepherd's crook was.

A small boy jumped up and said, "Yeah, it's the guy who steals the sheep."

BILLIE DICKE
OCEAN VIEW, HAWAII

VBS Truth

A vacation Bible school teacher saw one of her young students making faces at the other children.

She took the boy aside and reproved him: "Billy, when I was a child, I was told that if I made ugly faces, my face would freeze, and I would stay like that."

"Well, Mrs. Jones, you can't say you weren't warned." Billy replied.

GEORGE GOLDTRAP

Safe-Deposit Pages

A pastor asked a little girl, "So you attend Sunday school every Sunday?"

"Yes, sir," replied the girl.

"And you know your Bible?"

"Oh yes, sir."

"Could you tell me something that's in it?"

"I can tell you everything that's in it," the girl said. "My sister's pictures of her steady boyfriend are in it; all of our birthdays are in it; there's a lock of my hair in it; and mother's recipe for chocolate cake."

JIM REED

A Kid's Paraphrase

The children in the kindergarten class at St. Margaret Mary Catholic Church in Winter Park, Florida, put together their own version of the Lord's Prayer:

Our Father, who lives in heaven,
His name is special,
His world will come,
So we can check it out!
Let's play nice on earth,

Just like they play in heaven.
Please give us and we'll share
All our food, especially pizza.
And forgive us for being
Naughty sometimes,
And forgive everybody else, too.
Lead us away from the cookie jar
Before dinner,
And keep us safe from bad things.
We believe!!! (and we understand).

BOBBE LYON
MAITLAND, FLORIDA

Real Rejoicing

In Sunday school, the children were studying the parable of the prodigal son. The teacher asked, "What did the father say when he saw his son returning?"

A little girl smiled ear-to-ear, raised both tiny fists, and sang, "It's party time!"

DON WOOD
L'ANSE, MICHIGAN

"No, Henry. 'The Feeding of the Five Thousand' is not another one of the pastor's fish stories."

from *JoyfulNoiseletter.com*
© Dik LaPine.

Whatcha Gonna Do?

A mother was watching her four-year-old child playing outside in a small plastic pool half filled with water. He was happily walking back and forth across the pool, making big splashes. Suddenly, he stepped out of the pool, and began to scoop water out of the pool with a pail.

"Why are you pouring the water out, Johnny?" the mother asked.

" 'Cause my teacher said Jesus walked on water. And this water won't work," the boy replied.

REV. WOODY MCKAY
STONE MOUNTAIN, GEORGIA

Disney Version?

In Sunday school at Sheffield, Ontario, United Church, the children were talking about Bible stories that involved water. The teacher asked: "What about the man who was swallowed by the whale?"

A six-year-old child replied: "That was Pinocchio's dad!"

REV. TIM HAYWARD
SHEFFIELD, ONTARIO

Not Exactly

The Rev. Canon C. Frederick Barbee, editor of *The Anglican Digest*, was talking to the second-grade Sunday school class at Cathedral Church in Birmingham about Archbishop Cranmer's martyrdom under Queen Mary.

He asked the class if anyone knew Queen Mary's nickname. "Bloody Mary," one bright little boy answered.

"No," another boy quickly corrected him. "That's what my daddy has after church."

THE ANGLICAN DIGEST

What You Need to Know About Angels

"It's not easy to become an angel. First, you die. Then you go to heaven. Then you have to go through flight training. And then you've got to agree to wear those angel clothes."

LUKE, AGE 7

Four-year-old granddaughter Jennifer, whose father is a Presbyterian pastor, was walking down the street when they passed an elderly gentleman waiting at a bus stop.

The girl caught the man's attention, and he referred to her as "an angel."

Perturbed, Jennifer replied, "I am not an angel." She lifted up the back of her shirt and declared, "See, I don't have wings on my back!"

BOB WHITE
NAILSWORTH, ENGLAND

"I only know the names of two angels. Hark and Harold."

SUSAN, AGE 4

"Angels work for God and watch over kids when God has to go do something else."

THOMAS, AGE 8

"Angels don't wear halos anymore. I forget why, but scientists are investigating it."

GERTRUDE, AGE 9

Kyra Adell Champagne, age nine, is homeschooled by her mother in Jacksonville, Florida. Kyra followed instructions on a test and drew a straight line, a curved line, and a triangle. But when asked to draw an "angle," she drew an angel with a halo.

ADELL TALBOTT
SHELBYVILLE, KENTUCKY

"What I don't get about angels is why, when someone is in love, they shoot arrows at them."

LIZZIE, AGE 6

A Hand-y Observation

Little Bobby's grandmother took him to the park one Sunday afternoon. A fresh snow had fallen. His grandmother asked, "Have you learned in Sunday school that God painted this wonderful scene just for us to enjoy?"

Bobby replied, "Oh, yes. And just think! God did it with His left hand!"

"God's left hand?" the grandmother inquired.

"Well, I guess so," Bobby said, "because this morning we learned at Sunday school that Jesus sits on God's right hand."

REV. JOHN BURTON
IRVING, TEXAS

Further Angel Education

Sonny Garrett, columnist for *The Baxter Bulletin* of Mountain Home, Arkansas, collected some kids' comments on angels that were passed on by Jim Reed of Cotter, Arkansas.

"When an angel gets mad, he takes a deep breath and counts to ten. And when he lets his breath out, somewhere there's a tornado."

DANIEL, AGE 7

"Angels have a lot to do and they keep very busy. If you lose a tooth, an angel comes in through your window and leaves money under your pillow. Then when it gets cold, angels go north for the winter."

SARAH, AGE 6

"My guardian angel helps me with math, but he's not much good for science."

HARRY, AGE 7

"Angels don't eat, but they do drink milk from holy cows."

JERRI, AGE 5

"Some angels are in charge of helping heal sick animals and pets. And if they don't make the animals better, they help the kid get over it."

SARAH, AGE 7

"Angels live on cloud houses made by God and His Son, who's a very good carpenter."

SAMMY, AGE 7

from *JoyfulNoiseletter.com*
© Ed Sullivan.

"Knock, Knock."
"Who's There?"
"Buddy." "Buddy Who?"
"Every Buddy Needs
a Buddy."

God's Kids and Their Friends

Funny how an eight-year-old can't think of anything to say in his "thank-you" letter to grandma, but he can talk a mile a minute with his friends. Kids and friends are really a brilliant study in loyalty. Makes you wonder what was really meant when that teacher wrote, "Junior plays well with other children, but he needs to curb his enthusiasm for hugging our little girls."

Five-Year-Old Truth

Carol Peppler, secretary of Calvary Evangelical Lutheran Church, Belleville, Illinois, says the following story about her five-year-old grandson, Zack Halstead, made her think of the painting *The Risen Christ by the Sea* (see at www. joyfulnoiseletter.com):

Zack and his three-year-old friend, Joshua, were drawing with crayons at the kitchen table.

Zack's mother, Marge, and father, Bud, overheard Joshua telling Zack: "It makes Jesus happy when you share. If you don't share, it makes Jesus very sad. You don't want to make Jesus sad, do you?"

Marge hollered into the kitchen: "Zack, share your crayons!"

That evening, after saying his prayers in bed, Zack told his father: "You know, Daddy, Joshua's Jesus is sad all the time. But my Jesus is very happy!"

Friendly Friends

Mark E. Honstein, chaplain of the Lutheran Good Samaritan Society in Loveland, Colorado, took his wife out to a dinner theater for their anniversary. They left their four-year-old daughter, Amelia, with his parents, who live in the apartment above theirs.

While they were gone, Amelia got into her grandparent's refrigerator and spilled a big bowl of Jell-O on the kitchen floor.

Thinking she was in trouble, she ran downstairs to her parents' apartment to hide out. A pastor-friend happened to call Honstein, and Amelia answered the phone.

"Is your daddy home?" he asked.

"No," she replied, crying.

"Is your mommy home?" he asked.

"No," she replied still crying.

"Is anyone there with you?"

"No," Amelia sobbed, "it's just me and Jesus!"

The concerned pastor-friend then phoned Honstein's parents, and Amelia's grandmother went down to get her and assure her that everything was okay, and she'd make another bowl of Jell-O.

Later, Honstein was talking with Amelia about Jesus again, and asked her if she knew who Jesus is. She answered: "Yup. He is the pretend man that lives with us. But don't worry, Daddy, because He is not a stranger. I know His name."

from *JoyfulNoiseletter.com*
© Ed Sullivan.

Those Boyfriends

A Sunday school teacher asked her class to write essays on the story of Samson. One teenage girl wrote: "Samson wasn't so unusual. The boys I know brag about their strength and wear their hair long, too."

That John?

My four-year-old son and his sisters (ages eight and twelve) were having a discussion about the names of the books of the New Testament. My older daughter called out, "Matthew, Mark, Luke, and John."

My son asked, "John Smith, who goes to our church?"

My older daughter replied, "No, I think it's John the Baptist."

My son asked, "Does he go to our church, too?"

"No, we're Methodist," my eight-year-old daughter answered.

LANA CALVERY
GREENVILLE, TEXAS

Our Catholic Friends

"I am a church secretary in an evangelical church in western Pennsylvania. Sometimes I take my two kids to work with me. One day, I was on the phone with a fellow Sunday school teacher when the topic of Catholicism came up.

"We were discussing the tragic mindset of some people who were surprised that even Catholics were going to heaven along with us holy Protestants. After I hung up the phone, my eight-year-old daughter asked me what a Catholic was.

"My six-year-old son immediately told her: 'You know what it is! You know, what I have in my hair? A calf-lick!'"

JENNIFER RUNYAN
KNOX, PENNSYLVANIA

The Honest Lawn Boy

A young boy was walking down the street pushing a lawn mower. A priest who was out in his yard said, "Hi, son. Where are you going with the mower?" The boy said, "I'm trying to sell it. I want to buy a bicycle."

The priest said, "How much do you want for it? We may be able to use a mower around the yard here." The boy thought thirty dollars would buy him a bicycle, so he sold the mower to the priest for thirty dollars.

A couple of days later, the boy rode by the rectory on his new bike. The priest was out in the yard pulling on the cord, trying to start the mower. The boy said, "Oh Father, you have to cuss a little to get that mower started."

The priest replied, "I've been a priest twenty-five years, and I've forgotten how to cuss."

The boy said, "You keep on pulling that cord, and it'll come back to you!"

Mrs. Robert F. Sims
Eustis, Florida

10

THE FAMILY CIRCUS
by Bil & Jeff Keane

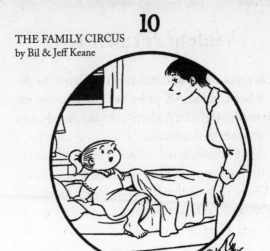

"What I like best about Easter Sunday is the candy, and Jesus not bein' dead anymore."

from *JoyfulNoiseletter.com*
© Bil Keane.

"How Come All the Big Stuff in the Bible Happened on a Holiday?"

God's Kids and Holy Days

It just can't be a coincidence that biblical high points are printed in red numbers on calendars, and we give gifts, scrounge for eggs, and light candles to celebrate them. Makes one remember the little boy who asked his daddy, "Did baby Jesus come down the chimney before or after the Grinch?"

Safety for Jesus

A little girl was fascinated by a nativity scene set up in her church. Asked by her mother, she was able to identify Mary, Joseph, the shepherds, and the animals in the stable.

"And what's that?" her mother asked, pointing to the manger.

"Oh, that's baby Jesus' car seat, Mommy!" the little girl said, proudly.

Fair Warning

A couple of weeks before Easter, a pastor was teaching a Sunday school class of small children about forgiveness and the story of the thief on the cross. Finally, she asked, "And what were Jesus' last words on the cross?"

A little boy raised his hand and in his deepest voice answered, "I'll be back!"

The Anglican Digest

The Missing Jesus

At Christmastime, a visiting family was driving around town looking at manger scenes. When they drove by the manger scene outside the Episcopal church, the five-year-old boy asked who the figures were.

"That is Mary, Joseph, and the baby Jesus in the manger," the mother explained.

Then they drove by a Methodist church, where the entire crèche was on display.

"Who are those guys?" the boy asked.

"Oh, those are the three wise men," the father said. "They are looking for the baby Jesus."

"Well, they won't find him there!" the boy exclaimed. "He's down at the other church!"

REV. WARREN J. KEATING
DERBY, KANSAS

Censorship Fashion

On Palm Sunday, all the children were gathered around the pastor for the children's sermon. The pastor noticed that one little girl was wearing a particularly pretty dress.

He leaned over and said, "That is a pretty dress, Kate. Is that your Easter dress?"

The little girl answered into the pastor's clip-on mike, "Yes, and my Mom says it's a [bleep] to iron."

GEORGE GOLDTRAP

You Asked for It!

On Easter Sunday, Rev. Karl R. Kraft of the First United Methodist Church of Mantua, New Jersey, walked through the congregation giving them an Easter "pep talk."

The pastor invited the congregation to sing and shout out whatever they felt would make them joyful on Easter, such as "Praise the Lord!" or "Thanks be to God!"

A small preschool boy shouted: "I want to go home!"

Maternity Kudos

A Sunday school class of first graders was asked by their teacher to write their own version of the Nativity. They had the familiar cast: Joseph, the three wise men, the star, and an angel propped up in the background.

Everything else was modernized. There were some bales of straw, behind which Mary was apparently in labor. Suddenly the "doctor" emerged from the "delivery room" with a big smile and exclaimed: "Congratulations, Joseph, it's a God!"

REV. FELIX A. LORENZ JR.
DEARBORN HEIGHTS, MICHIGAN

Whoops!

A father who rarely went to church decided to take his six-year-old boy to church on Easter Sunday. When they arrived at the church and sat in a pew, the boy looked around and asked in a loud voice: "Where are the Christmas trees that were here last time?"

JEFF TOTTEN

Naturally

At a church Christmas pageant, the little girl portraying Mary dropped the baby Jesus doll she was holding, and it bounced down the aisle crying "Mama, Mama." Later, a little boy wearing a bathrobe and a paper crown came out and announced, "We are the three wise men, and we are bringing gifts of gold, common sense, and fur."

BUD FRIMOTH

Christmas Spirit

"Love is what's in the room with you at Christmas if you stop opening presents and listen."

EIGHT-YEAR-OLD GIRL

A Promise Kept

One Christmas afternoon I went over to the church for a quiet visit before the crib. The infant Jesus was missing. None of the sisters knew what happened. Nor did any of the neighbors. We went in all directions. No sign of the baby.

Finally, one of the searchers spied a four-year-old boy pulling a brand new red wagon. In it was the baby Jesus from our crib.

The boy explained: "I promised Jesus if I got a wagon for Christmas, I would give Him the first ride."

MSGR. ARTHUR TONNE
JOKES PRIESTS CAN TELL

from *JoyfulNoiseletter.com*
© Doc Goodwin.

Your Answer?

For Christmas we had received a picture of Christ standing and knocking at a door, and we hung it on the wall in the living room. Our two granddaughters, Karen, then four, and Lori, three, were playing in the living room.

Lori kept getting up from her play to stand and look at the picture, then going back to play with her sister awhile, and going back to look at the picture again. Finally, Karen asked, "Lori, why do you keep looking at that picture all the time?"

Lori replied, "Isn't someone going to open the door?"

UNA BLOMQUIST
EDMORE, NORTH DAKOTA

As You Were

A member of University Baptist Church in Chapel Hill, North Carolina, Frank Fearrington took his two young grandsons to the church in late December to put away the ornaments and take down the Christmas tree. The boys began to race around the sanctuary, and Frank scolded them:

"You shouldn't do that, boys. This is God's house."
The four-year-old looked up innocently at Frank
and asked: "Doesn't God like little boys, Grand-
daddy?" With a shrug and a wave of his hand,
Frank signaled to the boys to carry on what they
were doing.

PEGGY E. YATES
DURHAM, NORTH CAROLINA

For Seven Days?

The week before Easter is known as Holy Week
because of its special significance to Christians.
During this past Holy Week, a first-grade teacher
at the local Lutheran school took great pains to
explain all the events in Jesus' life that led up to
the first Easter. She told them about Palm Sunday, and Good Friday, and finally Easter.

When she thought she had explained everything there was to know about that special week,
the teacher asked if the students had any questions.
One curious little boy raised his hand and asked,
"What happens if you don't want to be holy all
week?"

DANIEL HINTZ

"A great New Year's resolution for you would
be to set a better moral tone in kindergarten."

from *JoyfulNoiseletter.com*
© Ed Sullivan.

Away in a Manger

In preparation for Christmas, a Sunday school teacher told her children to write on small slips of paper the kind of gift the infant Jesus would like and could use. They were to drop these slips in a box near the classroom crib.

Some of the children misunderstood. Instead of the name of the gift, they put the gift itself in the box. In the box the teacher found a can of baby food, a small teddy bear, a toy truck, a tiny pair of mittens, and a disposable diaper.

At their classroom party, the children were to "show and tell" their gifts. The little girl who had given the diaper said: "Jesus was a real baby. Real babies need diapers."

MSGR. ARTHUR TONNE

Revised Version

A first-grade class presented a nativity play shortly before Christmas. When Joseph came to the inn and asked if there was room at the inn, the little boy playing the innkeeper replied, "You're lucky. We just had a cancellation."

GEORGE GOLDTRAP

Good News!

Easter was coming, and Joanne Hinch of Woodland Hills, California, was sitting at her kitchen table coloring Easter eggs with her son, Dan, three, and her daughter, Debby, two. She told her children about the true meaning of Easter, and taught them the traditional Easter morning greeting, "Christ is risen!"

The children planned to surprise their father, a Presbyterian minister, with this greeting on Easter Sunday morning by saying "He is risen!" as soon as he awoke. The next morning, bright and early, little Dan heard his father arising in the bedroom, and raced down the hallway shouting, "Daddy, God's back!"

A Heart Warmer

During an Easter service, as the pastor and the choir processed silently down the aisle carrying lighted candles, a small preschool boy became excited and burst out singing, "Happy Birthday to you."

REV. VERNON BABCOCK
FRANKLIN, OHIO

"No, I haven't been a good boy, but I now repent."

No Returns or Refunds

A child's letter to Santa Claus: "Dear Santa: Last Christmas I asked you for a baby sister. This Christmas I want you to take her back."

How about a Donkey?

A Sunday school teacher asked her small children what kind of animal Jesus rode when He came into Jerusalem on Palm Sunday.

A little boy had an immediate answer: "The Easter Bunny!"

REV. BARRY NEAL
CLAYSBURG, PENNSYLVANIA

Worry about Mary

Our youngest son was cast as Joseph in the children's Christmas pageant at church on Christmas Eve. As we drove to church that night through a blinding snowstorm, he worriedly exclaimed from the backseat: "What are we going to do if Mary doesn't get there?"

DR. R. ALAN STEWART
WILMINGTON, DELAWARE

When You Care Enough. . .

A little boy was asked in Sunday school what he was going to give his sister for Christmas.

"I don't know," he said.

"What did you give her last year?" the teacher asked.

"Chicken pox," he replied.

Baby Dishing

Each Advent season our family sets up our main nativity scene in the dining room with the stable and all the figures except that of baby Jesus. For safekeeping, I've always put the Jesus figurine in the china hutch until Christmas Eve, when it is added to the crèche.

When our daughter Katy was four years old, I overheard her gravely instructing her brother Andy, then two years old: "Now, Andy, this is Mary and Joseph; here are the shepherds and the wise men—and Jesus is in the china hutch waiting to be born."

CAROL SHUKLE
MOUND, MINNESOTA

Real Sacrifice

A mother was getting irritated with her five-year-old daughter, who wouldn't clean up her toys in the den.

"Mommy, I can't clean up in the den," the little girl said after her mother fussed at her for the third time.

"Why not?" the mother asked.

"Because I gave up cleaning for Lent," she replied.

SMILEY ANDERS

Country of Origin

A first-grade youngster in Toronto told her class that Santa Claus was from China. When the teacher asked her why she believed Santa lived in China, she replied that all of her gifts from Santa were marked "Made in China."

RICHARD KRUSE
TORONTO, ONTARIO

Ouch!

A department-store Santa Claus asked a little boy sitting on his lap: "What would you like for me to bring you for Christmas?"

The boy replied, "Don't tell me you didn't get my e-mail!"

ART POLISHUK
WEST CHESTER, PENNSYLVANIA

"Will God know it's me?"

from *JoyfulNoiseletter.com*
© Bil Keane.

"Since There Are No Holidays in August, Can We Have a Happy Hamsters Day?"

God's Kids and the Other Special Days

As if there are not enough red-letter days on the calendar, someone has suggested that we celebrate National Kids' Day. In a poll taken by Miss Murdy's fourth-grade class, it was decided that the following three suggestions were excellent ways of observing such a holiday: (1) The president should declare that Chuck E. Cheese pizza be substituted for broccoli surprise in the cafeteria; (2) Every little girl will hang her stocking on the TV set with care, and have every reason to believe that Justin Bieber soon will be there; (3) Each kid will produce a report card for his or her teacher, indicating whether she or he plays well with his or her pupils.

In Black and White

A little boy attended a wedding in church for the first time. "Why is the bride dressed in white?" he whispered to his mother.

His mother replied, "Because white is a symbol for purity, and it's the color of happiness, and today is the happiest day of her life."

"Then why is the groom wearing black?" the boy asked.

JASON GOLDTRAP
HAYNES CITY, FLORIDA

The Presence of Presents

Our son's third birthday fell on a Sunday, and while at church, I told him that when he got home he could open his presents.

At the end of the service, the pastor began his benediction: "Lord, we thank You for Your presence today."

My son turned to me and said, "Mom, the pastor thanked God for my presents!"

ANGIE BEACHY
FISHER, ILLINOIS

Red, White, and Blew Up

On the Fourth of July, my sixteen-year-old son, Ken, took my three-year-old grandson, Jeremy, to the backyard to shoot off bottle rockets into the night sky.

Jeremy had never seen fireworks before, and he rushed wide eyed back into the house. "Grandma," he said, "Uncle Ken took me outside, and he lit something, and he broke a star!"

PASTOR REBECCA KOIVU
CALUMET, MICHIGAN

"Dad, if I anoint your head with oil, will your cup run over?"

from *JoyfulNoiseletter.com*
© Ed Sullivan.

Surprise!

On a Mother's Day card, a seven-year-old girl wrote her mother: "Dear Mom, I'm going to make lunch for you on Mother's Day. It's going to be a surprise. P.S. I hope you like pizza and popcorn."

Paper or Plastic

On a Halloween afternoon, Rev. John Petramale, assistant pastor at St. Margaret Mary Catholic Church, purchased a few bags of goodies for trick-or-treaters, and wearing his clerical attire, moved through the checkout process at an Omaha supermarket.

A young grocery sacker eyed him enviously and said, "I really like your Halloween costume."

MSGR. ARTHUR TONNE

Fashion Show

During our church's Wednesday activities a week before Halloween, six-year-old Michael came to me to show off the neat biblical costumes which the children had made for Halloween—tunics, headdresses, etc.

He was really proud of them, and with wide eyes he said: "Yeah, these are the kind of clothes that the children wore when God was alive!"

REV. WARREN J. KEATING

Only the Best

Some children were acting out a wedding ceremony. The "priest" asked the "bride," "Do you take him for better or worse?"

"For better," the little girl said quickly.

The priest continued, "For richer or poorer?"

"For richer," stated the miniature bride.

Lincoln or Washington

An American boy was comparing holidays with a British boy. He observed, "It sure would be nice if we got a day off for all the presidents' birthdays like they do for your queen. Of course, then we would have a lot of people voting for a guy running for president who was born on July third or December twenty-sixth, just for the long weekend."

A Special Wedding Day

Little Tony was in his uncle's wedding. As he came down the aisle during the ceremony, he carefully took two steps, then stopped and turned to the crowd. When facing the congregation he put his hands up like claws and roared loudly. So it went, step, step, turn, roar, step, step, turn, roar, all the way down the aisle.

As you can imagine, the congregation was near tears from laughing. By the time little Tony reached the altar, he was near tears, too. When later asked what he was doing, the boy sniffed and said, "I was being the ring bear."

12

THE FAMILY CIRCUS
by Bil & Jeff Keane

"Adam and Eve were lucky. They didn't have any childhood diseases."

from *JoyfulNoiseletter.com*
© Bil Keane.

"Then He Stuck This Popsicle Stick Down My Throat"

God's Kids and the Medical Profession

The doctor told Tim's parents, "Don't be alarmed over your son's thumb-sucking, he'll grow out of it. Why I'd bet my MD degree on it." Well, that didn't calm Tim's folk's fears. So they try to sic the Great Physician on him. "Jesus doesn't want you to do that," Dad warned. It must be true that the all-knowing and all-seeing Creator knew this would be the case. Tim's dad better understood medicine vs. theology vs. a four-year-old's reasoning when he found the boy engaged in the forbidden activity down by the furnace in the basement. "Don't yell, Dad, you said God sees everything I do, well I can suck my thumb down here because He can't see down through the roof, three ceilings, and all the floors between us." Yeah, but what about X-ray vision?

Kyle's Shot

When my boys were three months and two years old, we headed to the doctor's office for Kyle's first "shot." Matthew watched with wide-eyed horror as his younger brother screamed while receiving the injection.

Later, at home for lunch, I asked Matthew to pray at our meal. He immediately folded his hands, bowed his head, and whispered, "Thank You, God, for Kyle's shot—and thank You, God, it wasn't *us*! Amen."

PASTOR YVONNE RIEGE
GOSHEN CITY, INDIANA

Internal Info

Rev. Gordon Wells and his wife Sue, of Granite-ville, Vermont, passed along this story:

We had been teaching our seven-year-old daughter the difference between the Old Testament and the New Testament. One day we were discussing how we digest food. We explained: "The food gets chewed in the mouth and is broken down some there, then it goes to the stomach and gets broken down further, then the final part of digestion happens in the large intestines and small intestines."

Our daughter promptly interrupted and said, "Oh you mean the Old Testament and New Testament."

An Observation

A mother who was seven months pregnant with her fourth child was undressing to take a shower when her five-year-old daughter entered the bedroom.

"Mommy, you're getting fat!" the little girl said.

"You're right, dear," the mother said. "Mommy has another baby growing in her tummy."

"I know," the little girl replied, "but what's growing in your butt?"

GEORGE GOLDTRAP

Just Say. . .

Sally Dillon of Timberville, Virginia, took her four-year-old son, Michael, to the surgeon's office for a physical before a hernia operation. As the doctor poked and prodded, the boy asked, "Are you going to cut my tummy while I am awake?"

"No," replied the surgeon. "We will put you to sleep first, and you won't feel anything."

"How will you do that?" the child asked.

"We will give you some drugs that will make you sleep," he answered.

The boy struggled to a sitting position and shook his finger under the surprised surgeon's nose. "Say NO to drugs!" he admonished the doctor.

"Would some sleeping medicine be okay, instead?" the doctor asked.

"Yeah, that would be fine," said Michael.

Seek and Ye Shall Find

Our five-year-old grandson, Chad, was in the living room while his dad was watching an open-heart surgery on TV. As the camera zoomed in on the open chest, Chad got closer and stared at the TV.

Then he said: "Dad, where is Jesus? If Jesus lives in our hearts, why can't I see Him?"

CAROL SALGAT
PRESCOTT, MICHIGAN

A Denture Tale

Rev. Elise L. Astleford of Battleground, Washington, passed on this story about a woman who took her little daughter with her while delivering lunches to the elderly shut-ins.

At one home, the woman found her daughter staring at a set of dentures soaking in a saucer. The little girl whispered to her mother, "The tooth fairy will never believe this!"

Rx for Embarrassment

After a four-year-old boy told his father that he had a stomachache, the father suggested: "That's because it's empty. You'd feel better if you had something in it." He gave the child a glass of juice.

A couple of days later, the family's pastor came by to visit the family. The pastor mentioned that he had a headache.

The little boy responded: "That's because it's empty. You'd feel better if you had something in it."

REV. WARREN KEATING
DERBY, KANSAS

That's Grandpa Love

When his bedridden grandfather died in a hospital, a four-year-old boy was told by his parents that he was going to heaven to be with Jesus.

The boy closely watched the bed where the body of his grandfather lay, and after some time asked, "When is Gramps going up?"

JEFF TOTTEN

Grandma's Not Well

Rev. Warren J. Keating of the First Presbyterian Church in Derby, Kansas, tells this story, which happened in the office of a family physician where Rev. Keating's wife works as nurse:

A farm family—the mother, her six-year-old son, and three-year-old daughter—came to see the doctor because all three of them had been ill with the flu. The grandmother accompanied them.

The doctor explained that the mother and children needed to rest because they were sick.

"My grandma is sick, too," the little boy said.

"No, your grandma is not sick," the doctor said.

"Oh yes she is," the boy said. "She's depressed."

The mother added, "Yes, the children have been praying for grandma and her depression."

The little boy turned to his grandma and said, "I'm sorry to tell you this grandma, but you're going to be depressed for six more months."

"Why do you say that, honey?" his grandma asked.

"Well," the boy said, "I've been praying for a calf for six months, and I just now got it."

Heaven Can Wait

A little girl's cat was struck by a car, and her father took him to the vet. When the father returned without the cat, the little girl asked, "Where is the kitty?"

The father told her he was in cat heaven.

"I thought he was dead," she replied.

JEAN SPENCER
CAMARILLO, CALIFORNIA

No Hankie Needed

Maureen and Joe Knodel took their three-year-old daughter, Bridget, with them to mass at St. Cecilia Church in Rockaway, New Jersey. When the time came to go forward for communion, Bridget walked with them, and the priest placed his hand on Bridget's head.

Later, Bridget asked her mother, "Why did he do that?"

"To bless you," replied her mother.

"Why?" asked Bridget. "I didn't sneeze."

SHARON AND ANDY FISHER
DENVILLE, NEW JERSEY

A Natural Question

My seven-year-old son had been terribly sick with the flu. While I was washing his face with a cold cloth for his fever, he asked, "Mom, does God have a mommy?"

I answered, "No, I don't think so, honey."

He then asked, "But if God doesn't have a mommy, who makes Him feel better when He's sick?"

DENISE MASLOWSKI
DULUTH, MINNESOTA

A Grandfather's Heart

When my small son's great-grandfather died at the age of ninety-nine, we told him that his grandpa went to be with Jesus. A rather perplexed look appeared on his young face.

A little later he asked me how great-grandpa (a tall, large man) could be in his heart. It dawned on me that Jesus was in my son's heart, and he was having trouble fitting in great-grandpa, too.

BECKY SPRUNGER
PANDORA, OHIO

Dr. What?

A university awarded a magazine religion writer an honorary doctorate of divinity.

A couple of days later, the man's four-year-old daughter was overheard telling her friends, "People now call my daddy 'Doctor Reynolds.'" She then added, "But Daddy's not the kind of doctor who will do you any good!"

ADAPTED FROM THE *Toronto Globe and Mail*

A Doc's Specs

My "flip-up" magnifying operating lenses never fail to provoke inquisitive stares from the little children at our post-service coffee hour. Victoria, age four, approached me and asked, "Why do you wear those funny glasses?"

I answered flippantly, "I wear them so that I can see when I stand on my head."

She quickly reported my answer to her coffee-sipping mother on the other side of the hall, then returned, and hands on hips, demanded, "Show me!"

Some of us never learn to tell the truth to children!

R. ALAN STEWART, DDS
WILMINGTON, DELAWARE

from *JoyfulNoiseletter.com*
© Doc Goodwin.

"Mom, When Am I Going to Be a Grown-up?"

God's Kids, the Future, and Everything Else

There are so many ways to measure your favorite kid's growth. Candles on her birthday cake and his height markings on the doorjamb are but two. One mom recently shared that one way she knew her child was "growing up" was by his nighttime prayers. It's amazing how much you can learn after the "Now I lay me downs" and

"God blesses." That same mother reported that one night her little Sammy began his prayer, "Dear Harold. . ." When questioned, he explained that in church we say, "Our Father, who art in heaven, Harold be thy name."

Not All Sixty-Six of 'Em

After church, a small boy announced to his mother: "When I grow up, I want to be a pastor. It's an easy job!"

"Why do you say that?" his mother asked.

"Because you only have to read one book," the boy replied.

REV. ROBERT M. THOMPSON
HICKORY, NORTH CAROLINA

Car Talk

Driving home from church one Sunday, a father asked his small son, "What do you think you will do when you grow up to be as big as I am?"

"Diet," the boy replied.

JOEL E. BAIR
GRAND RAPIDS, MICHIGAN

How's It Look?

After Marge Squire's Sunday school class at Hunter Community United Methodist Church in Franklin, Ohio, one youngster, Tyler Smiddy, ran up to his mother and exclaimed: "Guess what? I'm psycho!"

"What do you mean?" his mother asked.

"I'm psycho," little Tyler replied. "I can see the future."

REV. R. VERNON BABCOCK
FRANKLIN, OHIO

Better Start Figuring

Humorist George Goldtrap, enjoying his retirement, was riding a bike with his small grandson, Coleman, in Ormond-by-the-Sea, Florida. The boy was riding in an infant seat behind Goldtrap, his arms tightly around his grandfather's waist.

"Grandpa," the boy asked, "what are you going to be when you grow up?"

Goldtrap, hardly able to contain laughter, finally replied: "Well, Coleman, I really haven't given it much thought."

PEGGY GOLDTRAP

from *JoyfulNoiseletter.com*
© Ed Sullivan.

And the Other Seven?

A little boy told his pastor, "My mommy taught me three of the Ten Commandments: "Settle down." "Act your age." And "Take that out of your mouth."

REV. HARRY MAHONEY
DEDHAM, MASSACHUSETTS

Fishin' for the Truth

A little boy was taken on a weekend fishing trip with his father—a pastor—and several other fishermen. The first night, he listened to the anglers spin yarns around the campfire.

When they went to bed that night, the boy whispered to his father, "Dad, is it true that George Washington never told a lie?"

"Yes, son," the father replied, "but why do you ask?"

"Well, I was just thinking—he must never have gone fishing."

JIM REED
THE FUNNY SIDE OF FISHING

Oral Hygiene

Every school day morning, before he sends his two small children off to the bus stop to pick up the school bus, a father has some prayer time with the children. The father reminds the boy, seven, and the girl, six, to close their eyes and put their heads down during the prayer.

One morning, in the middle of the prayer, the father noticed that the boy was looking out the window.

"Please close your eyes and look down," the father requested.

"But, Dad," the boy protested. "Your breath smells so bad."

Sabbath Truth

Jimmy was on his way home one Sunday evening with a full string of catfish when he saw the town's preacher approaching him. Since there was no way to escape, Jimmy walked up to the pastor and said, "Reverend, see what these catfish got for biting worms on Sunday!"

JIM REED

Revised Fisherman's Version

When the preacher approached the boy who was fishing in the park pond, he said, "Young man, do you know the parables?"

"Yes, sir," quickly replied the lad.

"Which do you like best?"

The boy looked up and grinning, replied, "The one where everybody loafs and fishes."

JIM REED

Heaven's Paparazzi

A mother was concerned because thunderstorm clouds were forming and lightning was flashing one afternoon shortly before her eight-year-old daughter was to walk home a couple of short blocks from school.

The mother ran outside to meet her and saw her walking casually along the sidewalk. The girl stopped and smiled whenever lightning flashed.

"God's been taking my picture all the way home!" she told her mother excitedly.

SUSAN KAY SMITH
PORTAGE, MICHIGAN

Maybe Not a Lot

A Sunday school teacher said, "Johnny, do you think Noah did a lot of fishing when he was on the ark?"

"Naw," replied Johnny, "how could he with just two worms?"

JIM REED

Literal Translation

A small boy playing outdoors was using his mother's broom as a horse. When it got dark, he left the broom in the yard and went inside the house.

His mother, looking for the broom, asked him where it was outside in the yard; she asked him to go get it.

The boy was afraid of the dark and didn't want to go out.

"The Lord is out there, too," the mother assured him. "Don't be afraid."

The boy opened the front door cautiously and yelled, "Lord, if You're out there, please hand me the broom."

GEORGE GOLDTRAP

By Any Other Name?

When their daughter Debby was two years old, Joanne Hinch of Woodland Hills, California, and her husband, a Presbyterian minister, invited a Catholic priest to Sunday dinner.

While Debby helped her mother bake a cake for the dinner, they practiced saying their guest's name, Monsignor Keating. After much practice on Debby's part, it continued to come out "Monster Keating."

"Well, let's just call him Father Keating," her mother finally said.

That seemed fine with Debby, but that evening, shortly before dinner, she asked, "Well, isn't Mother Keating coming?"

Girl Talk

One day after vacation Bible school, two sisters, about four and six, were waiting for their ride home. Rev. Dennis Daniel of First Baptist Church of Fountain Hills, Arizona, said to them, "I sure wish I had two pretty daughters like you."

The oldest girl looked up and asked, "Are your daughters ugly?"

No Word for It

An associate pastor was talking about Jesus to a group of youngsters in preschool.

A little girl asked, "Is Jesus still alive?"

"Yes," the pastor replied.

"Then where is He?" the girl asked.

"He died, but He came back and now He is with God," the pastor replied.

"You mean He's still *alive*?" the girl asked.

"Yes, He is," the pastor said.

The little girl wiped her forehead with her hand in a gesture of relief and exclaimed, "Whew!"

REV. DENNY J. BRAKE
RALEIGH, NORTH CAROLINA

"Dad, you're in luck. I have some time free next Tuesday to play catch with you."

from *JoyfulNoiseletter.com*
© Dik LaPine.

No Fish in Heaven?

After hearing several boasting fishermen stretch the truth about their catches, a mother reminded her son that it's a sin to tell a lie.

On the next fishing trip with his father, the boy asked, "Dad, have you ever lied?"

"Well yes, I'm afraid I have," his father confessed.

"How about mother?"

"On occasion, if she felt the truth would hurt, I guess she lied," the father said.

"How about grandpa and grandma?"

"I suppose they're like the rest of us," the father said.

"Well," the boy said, "all I can say, it must be lonesome up in heaven with nobody but God and George Washington."

JIM REED
THE FUNNY SIDE OF FISHING

Chopper Humor

The pastor was seeing whether the first graders remembered the previous lesson he had taught. Unfortunately, he called on Christina, who had been absent for the lesson.

He asked her to recite the first commandment. In response to her blank look, he gave the child a helpful start. He prompted, "'I am the Lord your God.'"

No response.

Again he tried. "'I am the Lord your God. You shall not...'"

Still no response.

Yet again, "'I am the Lord your God. You shall not have false...'"

This time Christina's face lit up. "Teeth?" she asked hopefully.

What Else?

During an interactive sermon, Rev. Linda Baldock, pastor of the United Methodist Churches of Pembina, Joliette, and Humboldt in North Dakota and Minnesota, had one side of the church representing Pilate and his kingdom and the other Jesus and His kingdom.

"Where did Pilate live?" she asked.

"A palace," came the response.

"Where did Jesus live?" she asked.

"Wherever," came the response.

"What did Jesus wear?"

The response: "A tunic."

"And what did Pilate wear?"

Seven-year-old Reid answered: "A pilot suit."

You Asked!

Before his retirement, Rev. Paul Ard of Lawrenceville, Georgia, Presbyterian Church was having his last time with the children during the worship service. He told them that John 3:16 was the most important verse in the Bible.

He then asked if they knew John 3:16. They all nodded. Then he asked if anyone could say John 3:16. A little boy raised his hand.

"Good," Rev. Ard said. "Will you say John 3:16 for us all?"

The little boy proudly replied, "John 3:16!"

WOODY MCKAY JR.
STONE MOUNTAIN, GEORGIA

Home Sweet Home

A mother scolded her young son for being so unruly, and the boy rebelled. He got some of his clothes, his teddy bear, and his piggy bank and proudly announced, "I'm running away from home!"

The mother calmly asked, "What if you get hungry?"

"Then I'll come home and eat!" the boy replied.

"What if you run out of money?" she asked.

"I'll come home and get some!"

"What if your clothes get dirty?" she asked.

"Then I'll come home and let you wash them."

The mother shook her head and told her concerned husband, who had come in to see what the hassle was about: "This kid is not running away from home—he's going to college."

Prayer Changes Things

Pastor Les Nixon of the Outback Patrol National Headquarters in Georges Hall, Australia, reports that he knows the family and the home where this happened:

After a church meeting at night, a traveling

evangelist was invited to the family's home for dinner and to stay overnight. The husband and wife said they had only two bedrooms and asked the evangelist if he'd mind sleeping in the same room with their five-year-old lad.

"Not at all," the evangelist said. "I have children of my own."

The lad was sound asleep in one of the single beds. So the evangelist very quietly prepared for bed, then knelt to pray next to his own bed.

The lad woke up, and the evangelist saw him kneeling in prayer on the other side of his own bed, too.

The evangelist quietly complimented the lad for joining him in prayer. The boy simply replied, "It's okay, sir. But the potty's on this side of my bed."